From PROPHECY to Perfection

a Treasury of Christmas Devotions

by SUSAN SLADE
and SUSIE HALE

WJHP

Wyatt House Publishing
Mobile, Alabama

Copyright © 2024 by Reverend Susan R. Slade and Karen Sue Hale. https://www.preciousjewelsministries.com

All rights reserved. Permission is granted to copy or reprint portions for any noncommercial use, except they may not be posted online without permission.

Wyatt House books may be ordered through booksellers or by contacting:

WYATT HOUSE PUBLISHING
Mobile, Alabama 36695
www.wyattpublishing.com

Because of the dynamic nature of the Internet, any web address or links contained in this book may have changed since publication and may no longer be valid.

Cover design by: Mark Wyatt
Interior design by: Mark Wyatt
ISBN 13: 978-1-954798-19-9

This book is also available at amazon.com, barnesandnoble.com, and other online retailers.

Printed in the United States of America

Unless otherwise noted, Scripture quoted from Berean Study Bible. The Berean Bible (www.Berean.Bible) Berean Study Bible (BSB) © 2016, 2020 by Bible Hub and Berean.Bible. Used by Permission. All rights Reserved. Free downloads and licensing available. www.biblehub.com

Scripture quotations marked (ESV) taken from The Holy Bible, English Standard Version. ESV® Text Edition: 2016. Copyright © 2001 by Crossway Bibles, a publishing ministry of Good News Publishers. Used by permission.

Scripture quotations taken from the Amplified® Bible (AMPC), Copyright © 1954, 1958, 1962, 1964, 1965, 1987 by The Lockman

Foundation Used by permission. www.Lockman.org

Scripture quotations marked (NIV) taken from THE HOLY BIBLE, NEW INTERNATIONAL VERSION®, NIV® Copyright © 1973, 1978, 1984, 2011 by Biblica, Inc.® Used by permission. All rights reserved worldwide.

Scripture quotations marked (NLT) taken from *Holy Bible*, New Living Translation, copyright © 1996, 2004, 2015 by Tyndale House Foundation. Used by permission of Tyndale House Publishers, Inc., Carol Stream, Illinois 60188. All rights reserved.

Scripture quotations marked KJV taken from the King James Version, public domain.

Scripture quotations marked (AMP) taken from the Amplified® Bible (AMP),
Copyright © 2015 by The Lockman Foundation. Used by permission. www.Lockman.org

Scripture quotations taken from the Complete Jewish Bible (CJB), Copyright © 1998 and 2016 by David H. Stern. Used by permission. All rights reserved worldwide.

Scripture quotations marked (VOICE) taken from The Voice™. Copyright © 2008 by Ecclesia Bible Society. Used by permission. All rights reserved.

ACKNOWLEDGMENTS

First and foremost, we thank our Lord and Savior Jesus Christ for sustaining both of us through physical trials while completing this book project. As our "elevator speech" says, "God chose us to be His precious jewels. We overcome life's challenges through the grace of God in order to radiate the glory of God."

We thank our pastor, Ben Polson, for helping us with our website and input for this project. He and our church family come alongside us in many ways.

We thank Chrissy Thorpe for writing the foreword to this book and for her longtime friendship and prayer support.

We thank Mildred and Jimmy Garner for allowing Susie to come into their home to photograph a Nativity scene for the front cover. Mildred had a fantastic collection of Nativity scenes to choose from. The one pictured is carved wood and is from Germany.

We thank Richard Albin of Richard Wayne Photography for Photoshopping the photo of the Nativity on the front cover to have a starry background and then using Midjourney AI™ to make the Nativity come to life. We also thank him for the photos of us on the back cover.

We thank Susan's lifters who enable Susan to be in her power chair on a regular basis and especially for the photo shoot! Dana Carr, Chelsea Landsee, Zach Sullivan, and Nick Shepherd. We thank them for not only lifting Susan literally but for consistently encouraging us and lifting us up in prayer as well.

We thank our prayer partner, Missy Blanchard, our cherished, chosen sister in the faith, for consistently, fervently lifting us up to the Father concerning not only our ministry but our personal lives. Missy is an independent, licensed, and ordained minister through the National Association of Christian Ministers.

We thank Jennifer Staatz of Maker's Haven Shop for tailoring and even designing/engineering clothing to work with Susan's earth-suit. We are so blessed to have found a seamstress extraordinaire!

We thank our Generous Gems (monthly donors) who make it possible for us to self-publish books and whose generosity enables us to continue in ministry.

We thank our board members Dane and Dana Carr, Crystal Foster, Eric Little, and Nick Miller and our Treasurer Rick Ivey for their guidance and support.

SOLI DEO GLORIA!

FOREWORD

Susan and Susie have outdone themselves excavating the Christmas story from the entire Bible! At a time when Christmas stress can make you feel brainless, this delightful book, From Prophecy to Perfection, will refocus your perspective. Their fascinating study reveals the salvation message fully intertwined with the Christmas message, including the beginning and the end of the Bible. Your view of Christmas will broaden as you come to fully appreciate all that God, the Father, and Jesus, His Christ, accomplished in the background—and there is a lot of background—to the Christmas story. Susan and Susie have produced a comfort-giving, brain-stimulating, interest-holding devotional that you will look forward to reading again each year.

The full verses are printed, you don't even have to look them up, just find a place to snuggle up with this book. You can give it to yourself as a life-saving component of the top priority. Enjoy taking your time, savoring the real meaning of Christmas (it really is NOT just about our giving) while your mind decompresses, and your spirit gets fed. Merry Christmas to You!

Chrissy Thorpe

Chrissy Thorpe has been married to Sam, a college theology professor for 47 years. Their blessings include four children, their spouses, and 12 grandchildren. At age 53, Chrissy was able to return to college to earn a master's degree in Practical Theology and has since been writing and teaching. Her college research was published as a textbook, Studies in Christology and Pneumatology. She enjoys her family, making jewelry, playing the piano, swimming, writing, and talking on the phone to Susan while she does laundry and cooks. Chrissy's friendship with Susan began in 1992. Because of Susan's limited earth-suit (her term) and fertile mind, that association has caused much spiritual growth between the two of them. Susie came into Susan's life in God's perfect timing, providing her with the love and care she deserved, as well as a chance to write together fulfilling both their callings. They are God's Ladies of the Spirit! Their accomplishments under the most trying physical, emotional, and financial encumbrances are miraculous and inspiring.

DEDICATIONS

God created in me a love for Christmas and joy in celebrating Jesus and used people to foster that love and joy. I dedicate this book first to Jesus and then to the people He placed in my life:

- My mom, Beverly Slade. My favorite Christmas memory with Mom involves homemade chocolate chip cookies and a pair of Christmas bells we created out of two Styrofoam cups and purple wrapping paper with a purple ribbon on top. I don't remember what we used for the ringer, but I thought they were beautiful and that Santa would be pleased. We had such fun making them.
- Nana (Helen Young) called me her Christmas Eve gift because I was released from the NICU just in time for Christmas 1966. She and her mom, Granny Henley, and Grannie Slade because their love of all things Christmas and especially nativities has made me continue to enjoy Christmas with a childlike wonder to this day—excited and giddy.
- My bonus parent, Becky Slade, who brought sunshine and joy into our lives and especially to my dad at Christmas, and her mother Grammy Neumeyer who had a collection of Christmas villages which family added to each year. She loved people with her gift of hospitality during the holidays.
- George and Patti Hearne, my bonus parents during my teenage years at boarding school, who nurtured my love of Jesus. Through their lives I saw that

the Christmas Spirit should live in our hearts every day of the year, not just for a season.

- Evans and Janelle Sirois who exude the Spirit of Christmas every day and adopted me into their family while I was away at college.

Susan

I dedicate this book to my dad who wrote "from Santa" on the gift tags of presents he chose which were usually something wonderful like the Purple Stingray Bicycle with a banana seat in third grade or my own set of golf clubs in a rolling golf bag when I was eighteen. He took us out to look at Christmas lights most years, which I thoroughly enjoyed. He is in the presence of Jesus now and has the joy of celebrating Christmas with his Savior.

Susie

Our desire is that this book encourages you (and us) to be living Christmas gifts of the love Jesus demonstrated through His incarnation every day of our lives on earth. Let Paul's description of our faith be evident to all who meet us: "Christ in you, the hope of glory" (Colossians 1:27b).

In His love,
Susan and Susie

PREFACE: GETTING MORE FROM THIS BOOK

We are not aware of another Christmas devotional book that begins with the Old Testament Messianic prophecies and their fulfillment in the person of Jesus Christ. We set out to bring the reader a deeper understanding of God's perfect plan for redemption and how it was completely fulfilled by His Son, Jesus. Here are some suggestions on how to go deeper in your experience with Jesus as you use this book:

1. We purposely did not designate certain days for reading each page. You may wish to read several pages at once, especially if you come to a poem. Or you may wish to really study each page and take time to ponder it. The rate at which you read is up to you, your schedule, and your needs at the time.

2. We quoted each focal scripture verse but suggest that you open your Bible or your Bible App, as the case may be, and read the entire passage to understand the context.

3. You may also want to look up any cross references that we did not quote in full. A short devotion does not lend itself to exploring fully every cross reference.

4. We purposely left blank space at the end of each devotion. Use this space for your own notes, poems,

drawings, insights, or whatever helps you focus your mind on Jesus.

5. If you have children or even if you don't, think about how you would explain the content of each devotion to a first grader, or sixth grader, or pre-school child. This will not only enhance your understanding of it by forcing you to break it down into its simplest form, but you will be prepared if a child asks you a question related to the devotion. Children often ask unusually profound questions.

6. We have included opportunities for worship experiences. If you are reading this in print format, please take a few moments to type the URLs into your browser on the computer or phone and listen to the songs. Keep in mind that web addresses sometimes change, but you can find most of these songs on YouTube. They are included not only for your enjoyment but because they will enrich your understanding of the message.

7. You may want to set aside a "date" with the Lord. Plan a time to take this book, your Bible, and maybe a notebook to a quiet place and spend an hour alone with Jesus. It can be a beautiful outdoor setting or a quiet coffee shop, just someplace you will not be disturbed. Read, pray, sing, worship, and most importantly listen to the Holy Spirit. You may think you don't have an extra hour, but the refreshment you gain by spending time with the Lord will invigorate you to complete your normal tasks.

8.   We have provided an index that lists all the scripture verses quoted or referenced in book of the Bible order to enable you to find a particular devotion if you are studying or teaching on one of those verses or passages.

Susan Slade and Susie Hale

TABLE OF CONTENTS

Acknowledgments	5
Foreword	7
Dedications	9
Preface: Getting More From This Book	11
Philippians 2:5-8: *Christmas Reflection*	19
Revelation 13:8- *Messiah: Incarnation and Crucifixion Planned Before Creation*	20
Genesis 3:14-15- *Messiah First Promised*	22
Genesis 3:15- *Messiah Promised*	24
Genesis 12:3- *Messiah to Be of Abraham's Seed*	26
Genesis 17:19 - *Messiah to Be Descendant of Isaac Specifically*	29
Psalm 46:10 - *A Christmas Prayer*	32
Numbers 24:17a, and 19a- *Messiah: The Star is Born*	34
Genesis 49:10- *Messiah: The Lion of Praise*	36
2 Samuel 7:12-13- *Messiah: Heir to David's Throne*	38
Psalm 103:19- *God's Sovereignty Seen in the Women of Christmas*	41

Psalm 2:7- *Messiah is God's Own Son*	*43*
Isaiah 7:14- *Messiah Will Be Born to a Virgin*	46
Isaiah 9:6-7- *Messiah: He Will Be Called by God's Names*	*49*
Micah 5:2- *Messiah to be Born In Bethlehem*	51
Micah 5:2- *Messiah is Eternal*	53
Luke 1:13-15- *Barren No More*	56
Luke 1:38- *Mary to Carry Messiah*	58
Luke 1:38 - *Tender Surrender*	61
Luke 1:41-45- *John Jumps for Joy*	63
Luke 1:44- *Unborn Baby's Praise*	65
Luke 1:46-48- *Humble Servant Magnifies the Lord*	68
Galatians 4:4-5- *Incarnation In A Nutshell,*	*70*
Isaiah 7:14- *Emmanuel: Part 1*	73
Matthew 1:23- *Emmanuel: Part 2*	75
Matthew 1:21- *What's in A Name?*	*77*

Luke 2:4-7- *As A Baby, He Came*	79
Luke 2:8-12- *Shepherds Shaking in Their Sandals*	81
Luke 2:10-11- *Rejoice: The Redeemer is Finally Here!*	84
Luke 2:15-16- *Shepherds Seek Swaddled Savior*	87
Luke 2:15-20- *Shepherds Herald Good Shepherd's Arrival*	90
Luke 2:21-24- *Redeemer Redeemed*	93
Luke 2:21-24- *Redeeming the Long-awaited Redeemer*	94
Luke 2:28-32- *The Light*	97
Luke 2:36-38- *Anna: Intercessor, Prophetess, Evangelist*	99
Matthew 2:10- *Star Gazers*	101
Matthew 2:23- *He Shall Be Called A Nazarene*	104
Hebrews 7:25- *Christmas Contemplation*	107
Isaiah 9:6-7- *Christmas*	110

Jewels of Salvation	111
Believers' Benefits	114
Dictionary of "Susanisms"	116
Index of Scripture Quoted or Referenced	118
Notes	123
Bibliography	124
About the Authors	125
About Precious Jewels Ministries	127

Let this mind be in you which was also in Christ Jesus: Who, existing in the form of God, did not consider equality with God something to be grasped, but emptied Himself, taking the form of a servant, being made in human likeness. And being found in appearance as a man, He humbled Himself and became obedient to death—even death on a cross.

Philippians 2:5-8

CHRISTMAS REFLECTION

Reflect this year at Christmas on what the Lord has done for us.
He gave up Heaven's glory to walk on this earth's dust.
As a tiny baby, placed Himself in mortals' hands.
He could have trod the streets of gold,
but chose to walk in sand.

He spent His life in service to those who should have served:
Then He hung upon the cross and took what we deserved.
So, as we think of what He gave to us by coming here,
Let us purpose in our hearts to live differently next year.
May our resolution be commitment to our Lord,
Renewed determination to live according to His word.

MESSIAH: INCARNATION AND CRUCIFIXION PLANNED BEFORE CREATION

Through Him all things were made, and without Him nothing was made that has been made. In Him was life, and that life was the light of men.

John 1:3-4 (BSB)

. . . the book of life of the Lamb slain from the foundation of the world.

Revelation 13:8b (KJV)

Christmas begins with creation and the fall of man. This idea is not original with us. We read a blurb on the "Sounds of the Season" TV channel that said glass ornaments originated to replace fresh apples placed on the tree to symbolize the forbidden fruit Adam and Eve ate in the Garden of Eden! The entire Trinity—God the Father, Jesus the Son, and the Holy Spirit—were present at the creation of the world. In fact, according to the Gospel of John, Jesus created everything. Jesus our Savior, the Messiah the Jews had waited for, knew even before He created Adam and Eve that they would eat the forbidden fruit. Even so, He breathed life into them knowing that in the fullness of time, He would be born as a human child, born so that He could die an agonizing death in our place on the cross. Since Jesus was Creator, present when woman was formed from man's rib, we love the lyrics by Michael Card that state, "No fiction as fantastic and wild, A mother made by her own child."

God knew He would create human beings from the dust of the earth. He knew we would have limited capacity to understand Him. He knew before they were even formed that Adam and Eve would disobey Him leading to death. However, He also had a redemption plan to rescue fallen humans before all of that occurred. It is beyond our ability to truly grasp all the "why's" of God's ways. We accept that He is God, and we are not. "For as the heavens are higher than the earth, so My ways are higher than your ways and My thoughts than your thoughts" (Isaiah 55:9). Jesus was "slain from the foundation of the world" in the sense that God had already planned the cross as believers' redemption before He created the first man. Yes, this is a difficult concept to grasp, but we accept it by faith.

Take a moment to reflect on the enormity of creation and the power of our Creator. Chew on the idea that Jesus knew He would ultimately be born to die even as He was forming those for whom He would die. Thank the Lord for the ultimate Christmas gift, the Savior born in Bethlehem!

Father, we thank You for creating us, breathing life into us. Thank You for planning for our salvation before we even knew we were lost. Thank You, Jesus, for becoming small enough for us to understand You, being born as a human baby, and growing up to die in our place on the cross.

MESSIAH FIRST PROMISED

The Lord God said to the serpent, "Because you have done this, you are cursed more than all the cattle, And more than any animal of the field; On your belly you shall go, And dust you shall eat all the days of your life. "And I will put enmity (open hostility) between you and the woman, And between your seed (offspring) and her Seed; He shall [fatally] bruise your head, And you shall [only] bruise His heel."

Genesis 3:14-15 (AMP)

But when the time had fully come, God sent His Son, born of a woman, born under the law, to redeem those under the law, that we might receive our adoption as sons.

Galatians 4:4-5

This is why the Son of God was revealed, to destroy the works of the devil.

1 John 3:8b

God showed up for their evening walk but found Adam and Eve hiding from Him. God, knowing what had happened, asked Adam three questions: How do you know you are naked? Who told you? Did you eat from the tree of the knowledge of good and evil? Thus, ensued the first "blame game." Adam blamed the woman and ultimately God by pointing out that God had given him this "helper." However, God had told Adam directly the command to not eat of the tree, so he should have known better than to participate in eating the fruit when Eve gave it to him. Then God turned to Eve and asked her what she did. She blamed the serpent (really Satan, the enemy of God and all humankind,) saying he deceived her. After hearing His family's case, God turned to the serpent and said, "For this you are cursed, crawl on the ground and eat dust all the days of your life." God continued with the curse of the serpent; but in so doing, He was giving Eve the first prophecy concerning the Savior, the Messiah, to come. Yes, snakes (serpents) bite the heel and we stomp their heads; but there is more to this prophecy. Satan is the enemy of humanity, constantly trying to prevent people from having a right relationship with their Creator. Crucifixion is one of the few forms of execution that "bruises the heel" as the spike is driven through the feet and the heels pushed hard against the cross. But as Jesus' heels were bruised, He was delivering the deathblow to Satan's head. Satan is truly a "dead devil walking." Eve and Adam were the first humans to hear this promise that Satan would ultimately be destroyed by Eve's Seed (singular) which would be Jesus. Usually "seed" denotes sperm, but it was by the woman's seed that deliverance would come. Mary conceived Jesus by the Holy Spirit without the normally necessary benefit of a human man's sperm, so Jesus was Mary's Seed and ultimately that of Eve.

Father, thank You for the record of the Messianic Prophecies in the Old Testament which enable us to see their fulfillment in the New Testament account of Jesus's incarnation.

And I will put enmity between you and the woman, and between your seed and her seed. He will crush your head, and you will strike his heel.

Genesis 3:15

And I will put enmity (open hostility) Between you and the woman, And between your seed (offspring) and her Seed; He shall [fatally] bruise your head, And you shall [only] bruise His heel.

Genesis 3:15 (AMP)

MESSIAH PROMISED

The serpent was beautiful and beguiling,
And the woman was deceived.
He told them the fruit would make them wise,
A half-truth they chose to believe.
Because they listened to someone other than God,
A curse came upon them and the earth.
Men would have to work hard to provide,
And women would have pain in childbirth.
The serpent on his belly would crawl,
But God gave them a promise that day.
Although the Deceiver would bruise man's heel,
Eve's Descendant would purchase the way
To defeat Satan once and for all
By fatally crushing his head.

Jesus' feet were bruised upon the cross,
But He conquered Satan once for all
WHEN HE ROSE UP FROM THE DEAD!

MESSIAH TO BE OF ABRAHAM'S SEED

I will bless those who bless you and curse those who curse you; and all the families of the earth will be blessed through you.

Genesis 12:3 (God speaking to Abraham)

So also, "Abraham believed God, and it was credited to him as righteousness." Understand, then, that those who have faith are sons of Abraham. The Scripture foresaw that God would justify the Gentiles by faith, and foretold the gospel to Abraham: "All nations will be blessed through you." The promises were spoken to Abraham and to his seed. The Scripture does not say, "and to seeds," meaning many, but "and to your seed," meaning One, who is Christ.

Galatians 3:6-8, 16

This is the record of the genealogy of Jesus Christ, the son of David, the son of Abraham:

Matthew 1:1

God told Abraham that through him all nations (not just the Jews) would be blessed. He further clarified that this promise would come through Sarah's child and not that of her handmaid (Genesis 17:15-19). When God told Abraham Sarah would bear a son, "Abraham fell facedown. Then he laughed and said to himself, 'Can a child be born to a man who is a hundred years old?

Can Sarah give birth at the age of ninety?'" (Genesis 17:17). It is important to note that Jesus descended from Isaac, not Ishmael, because God specifically chose Isaac to be the "son of promise." The "seed" or "descendant" of Abraham through whom all nations would be blessed was Jesus according to Galatians 3:16. An important aspect of the Gospel is that Christ did not come to redeem only the Jews but to die for the Gentiles as well because God had promised Abraham that ALL nations would be blessed. According to Galatians 3:29, those who trust in Jesus are Abraham's descendants, not through his blood line but through sharing the same faith Abraham demonstrated.

Galatians 3:29 And if you belong to Christ, then you are Abraham's seed and heirs according to the promise.

Jesus was a descendant of Abraham through both Mary's lineage and that of his adopted father, Joseph. We, too, are counted as descendants of Abraham if we have faith in Jesus. It was not Abraham's goodness or even his obedience that made him righteous. It was his faith in God, the fact that he believed the promise God gave to him even though it seemed impossible. Note that Abraham ROFL (rolled on the floor laughing) when God told him 90-yr-old Sarah would bear a son (Abraham laughed even before Sarah did). However, ultimately, he believed God.

Father, help us to have faith like Abraham who was willing to sacrifice Isaac because he believed God would keep His promise by raising Isaac from death (Hebrews 11:17-19).

MESSIAH TO BE DESCENDANT OF ISAAC SPECIFICALLY

But God replied, "Your wife Sarah will indeed bear you a son, and you are to name him Isaac. I will establish My covenant with him as an everlasting covenant for his descendants after him."

Genesis 17:19 (see also Genesis 21:12)

This is the record of the genealogy of Jesus Christ, the son of David, the son of Abraham: Abraham was the father of Isaac...

Matthew 1:1-2a

By faith Abraham, when he was tested, offered up Isaac on the altar. He who had received the promises was ready to offer his one and only son, even though God had said to him, "Through Isaac your offspring will be reckoned." Abraham reasoned that God could raise the dead, and in a sense, he did receive Isaac back from death.

Hebrews 11:17-29

God has always been about the details. God was very specific with Abraham. He made it clear that his family line—descendants like the number of the stars or the grains of sand, and the Descendant through whom the entire world would be blessed—would come through Isaac, not Ishmael. Abraham rolled on the floor laughing when God told him Sarah would have a child (Genesis 17:17). Later, Sarah laughed, too. Therefore, God (who has a sense of humor) told them to name the child Isaac meaning "he laughs". However, when the Lord told Abraham to offer his son, Isaac, as a burnt offering, Abraham (who had never heard of God raising someone from the dead) reasoned in his mind that if Isaac was God's choice to bring about descendants for him, that God must plan on raising him from the dead. Abraham got as far as tying Isaac to the altar and raising the knife above his chest when the Angel of the Lord stopped him! Isaac must have had faith as well because he was a teenager or young man and could have resisted his 100+ year old father, but he submitted to his father and allowed himself to be tied to an altar. Abraham was willing to obey God and sacrifice his son; but God provided a ram stuck in a thicket to replace Isaac, which is a picture for us of the fact that God sacrificed His only begotten Son on the cross to replace sinners (including us) who should have died there. The Messiah would be a descendant not just of Abraham, but specifically through Isaac.

If God has called you to a specific purpose, God will enable you to fulfill that purpose. Susan is fulfilling her calling to be God's megaphone by speaking and writing to share the Good News. If she can answer God's call and fulfill her purpose from her bed and her power chair, the rest of us are without excuse. Have faith like Abraham that God is able to perform through you that which He has called you to accomplish.

Father, when our faith wavers, remind us that there is no record of someone being raised from the dead before Abraham's time, but he believed You could and would do just that if he killed Isaac as a sacrifice. Help us to follow in the footsteps of the Father of Faith, Abraham, and have unwavering trust in You. Help us to believe like Sarah who carried a baby to term at 90+ years old that You will sustain us! Lord, strengthen our faith!

"Be still and know that I am God; I will be exalted among the nations, I will be exalted over the earth."
Psalm 46:10

"Cease striving and know that I am God; I will be exalted among the nations, I will be exalted in the earth."
Psalm 46:10 (NASB)

A Christmas Prayer

Dear Father,

It's Christmas time again,
and there is so much to distract me.
there's a rehearsal, a musical,
or a party almost every night.
There are presents that need to be purchased,
and, of course, they'll need to be wrapped.
And with all this hustle and bustle,
I long for that "long winter's nap."
It's Christmas time again,
and I'm feeling just exactly
like I need to sprout some wings and fly
so that I might
keep up with the schedule before me
and make it to each thing on time.

I covet just ten precious minutes
to sit and have peace of mind.

Slow me down.
Help me be still
and to know that You are Lord.
Help me make
the time each day
to meditate on Your word.
Focus me
Your will to see
and draw me near to You.
Be my guide
close by my side
In all that I say and do.

Amen

MESSIAH: THE STAR IS BORN

Your descendants will be like the dust of the earth, and you will spread out to the west and east and north and south. All the families of the earth will be blessed through you and your offspring.

Genesis 28:14 (God speaking to Jacob)

I see him, but not now; I behold him, but not near. A star will come forth from Jacob, and a scepter will arise from Israel . . .

. . . A ruler will come from Jacob.

Numbers 24:17a, 19a

Abraham was the father of Isaac, Isaac the father of Jacob . . .

Matthew 1:2a

"I, Jesus, have sent My angel to give you this testimony for the churches. I am the Root and the Offspring of David, the bright Morning Star."

Revelation 22:16

Again, we see God's attention to detail. Jacob had a twin named Esau who should have received the birthright to be Isaac's heir, but through deception, Jacob was the one Isaac blessed which led to his being in the lineage of Jesus. The Old Testament writers under the influence of the Holy Spirit prophesied that a Star would be born as one of Jacob's descendants. This Star is Jesus who is brighter than any star in the heavens and will not fade like the so-called stars in Hollywood. This Star shines brightly throughout the ages and will be the Brightness that lights up the New Jerusalem: "There will be no more night in the city, and they will have no need for the light of a lamp or of the sun. For the Lord God will shine on them," (Revelation 22:5a). This brightness, this radiance may have been the "star" the wisemen followed as some scholars believe that star to be the Shekinah glory of God!

Jesus is the Light, but He desires that light to shine through each believer. Jesus said, "I am the light of the world. Whoever follows Me will never walk in the darkness, but will have the light of life" (John 8:12) and, "You are the light of the world. A city on a hill cannot be hidden" (Matthew 5:14). Have you been trying to hide your light? Be bold in sharing the Gospel to people who are walking in darkness. Be a beacon of light and shine for Jesus!

Father, thank You for placing the light of life within us. Help us to shine brightly for You!

Worship the Star with CeCe Winans singing "Jesus, You're Beautiful": https://www.youtube.com/watch?v=pAHmf9qIXos

Worship with 5-yr-old Caleb Serrano singing "This Little Light of Mine": https://www.youtube.com/watch?v=4BLDEIFCL4M

MESSIAH: THE LION OF PRAISE

The scepter will not depart from Judah, nor the staff from between his feet, until Shiloh[H7886] comes and the allegiance of the nations is his.

Genesis 49:10

Abraham was the father of Isaac, Isaac the father of Jacob, and Jacob the father of Judah and his brothers. Judah was the father of Perez and Zerah by Tamar, Perez the father of Hezron, and Hezron the father of Ram.

Matthew 1:2-3

For it is clear that our Lord descended from Judah, . . .

Hebrews 7:14a

Then one of the elders said to me, "Do not weep! Behold, the Lion of the tribe of Judah, the Root of David, has triumphed to open the scroll and its seven seals.

Revelation 5:5

> H7886 shee-lo' – a masculine proper name meaning Shiloh. It is a noun meaning *whose it is* or *he whose it is (Genesis 40:10).* (1)

Shiloh—He whose it is—is Jesus since "All things were created through Him and for Him" (Colossians 1:16b). Jesus is the creator and owner of everything on earth. Why do we call Jesus the "Lion of Praise" in our title? Judah's name meant "praise." Judah was not the most upright character in the lineage of Christ. He intermarried with Canaanite women. He refused to give his third son Shelah in levirate marriage to his daughter-in-law Tamar after his first two sons died (Genesis 38). Then he unwittingly hired Tamar who was disguised as a prostitute, had relations with her, and fathered the twins Perez and Zerah. It was through Perez, the son Judah had with his daughter-in-law, that the Messianic line continued. Tamar is one of the five women listed in Matthew's genealogy of Jesus. Judah and Tamar both messed up and broke the Law. However, God still used them in the earthly lineage of His Son, Jesus!

You may argue that God could not possibly use you for His glory because of some heinous sin in your past. Not true! Once you have trusted Jesus as your Savior and Lord and committed the rest of your life to His service, God will glorify Himself through you. The night Susie's husband left her, she thought, "God can never use me again because I will be divorced." WRONG! God led her to teach in a Christian school and now she is working in full-time ministry as the Vice-President and Secretary of Precious Jewels Ministries. Ask the Lord how He wants to use you. Then pursue that goal wholeheartedly trusting that He will bring it about!

Father, thank You for not abandoning us when we fall short of Your glory. Thank You for forgiving and cleansing us when we confess our sins to You (1 John 1:9).

MESSIAH: HEIR TO DAVID'S THRONE

And when your days are fulfilled and you rest with your fathers, I will raise up your descendant after you, who will come from your own body, and I will establish his kingdom. He will build a house for My Name, and I will establish the throne of his kingdom forever.

2 Samuel 7:12-13 (God speaking to David)

Then a shoot will spring up from the stump of Jesse, and a Branch from his roots will bear fruit. The Spirit of the LORD will rest on Him—the Spirit of wisdom and understanding, the Spirit of counsel and strength, the Spirit of knowledge and fear of the LORD. And He will delight in the fear of the LORD.

Isaiah 11:1-3

Behold, the days are coming, declares the LORD, when I will raise up for David a righteous Branch . . .

Jeremiah 23:5a

Salmon was the father of Boaz by Rahab, Boaz the father of Obed by Ruth, Obed the father of Jesse, and Jesse the father of David the king.

Matthew 1:5-6a

The gospel He promised beforehand through His prophets in the Holy Scriptures, regarding His Son, who was a descendant of David according to the flesh.

Romans 1:2-3

God promised King David that the throne would continue in his family through One who would reign forever. David took Bathsheba to be his wife after he committed adultery with her and orchestrated having her husband, Uriah, put on the front lines to be killed in battle—in essence David had Uriah murdered. Their son, Solomon, built the first temple, but Solomon eventually died. The One whose throne would be established forever would be the Messiah, Jesus, who was a direct descendant of David through both his mother Mary and his earthly father, Joseph. There has not continually been a descendant of David on Israel's throne throughout earthly history. However, the Messiah's reign is eternal: "The kingdom of the world has become the kingdom of our Lord and of His Christ, and He will reign forever and ever" (Revelation 11:15b).

It is easy to skip over the genealogies in the Bible, but we have learned so much by reading them carefully and even looking up the people listed in cross references. The genealogies of Jesus in Matthew and Luke are not just there to prove He was descended from all these people. There is much to learn from them. Look at the women listed in Matthew's genealogy. If you have ever felt unworthy to be of use to God, look at Tamar who lured her father-in-law Judah to sleep with her, Rahab who was known as a harlot, Ruth who was from Moab, Bathsheba who was David's mistress—Jesus's grandmothers!

Father, we thank You for changing us to make us useful in Your kingdom!

Worship the King of kings by listening to "The Hallelujah Chorus" from Handel's "Messiah": https://www.youtube.com/watch?v=9jvsK798Lbs

The LORD has established His throne in the heavens,
And His sovereignty rules over all.
Psalm 103:19 (NASB)

GOD'S SOVREIGNTY SEEN IN THE WOMEN OF CHRISTMAS

Eve ate the fruit because she was deceived,
    but God already had a plan in place.
The serpent would bruise the heel of her Seed,
    but her Seed would stomp Satan's face.
Sarah was barren and came up with a plan
    to have Hagar bear Abraham a son.
But God said to Abraham, you don't understand;
    Sarah's son will be the chosen one.
Tamar pretended to be a prostitute
    and by her father-in-law, bore a son.
Although her ways were of ill repute,
    God prevented Judah's line from being done.
In Jericho, Rahab was known as a harlot,
    but she hid the spies Joshua sent.
Our sovereign Lord saved her from a tight spot:
    the rest of her days as a Jew were spent.
Rahab had Boaz by Salmon of Judah's line.
Boaz redeemed and married Moabitess Ruth
Who was loyal to Naomi with determined mind.

She was the grandmother of King David in truth.
Bathsheba was King David's mistress,
and he even had her husband killed.
But God in mercy forgave their big mess,
and her son Solomon the king's shoes filled.
Esther was a simple young Jewish girl,
but God raised her up to be queen of Persia.
With bravery to make your head swirl,
she saved her nation from a cruel plot's inertia.
Elizabeth, like Sarah was barren and old.
Her husband prayed, incense rising higher,
An angel appeared and their baby foretold,
a baby named John, forerunner of Messiah.
Mary was a peasant girl, but favored;
for God chose her to bear His Son.
Each moment surrounding His arrival she savored,
for her baby was the Promised One.
Anna, a widow, had served in the temple
and had longed to see the Anointed.
When she saw Baby Jesus, so tiny and simple,
others toward the Messiah, she pointed.

MESSIAH IS GOD'S OWN SON

I will proclaim the decree spoken to Me by the LORD: "You are My Son; today I have become Your Father.

Psalm 2:7

And now we proclaim to you the good news: What God promised our fathers He has fulfilled for us, their children, by raising up Jesus. As it is written in the second Psalm: 'You are My Son; today I have become Your Father.'

Acts 13:32-33

The Son is the radiance of God's glory and the exact representation of His nature, upholding all things by His powerful word. After He had provided purification for sins, He sat down at the right hand of the Majesty on high. So He became as far superior to the angels as the name He has inherited is excellent beyond theirs. For to which of the angels did God ever say: "You are My Son; today I have become Your Father"?

Hebrews 1:3-5

He will be great and will be called the Son of the Most High. The Lord God will give Him the throne of His father David.

Luke 1:32

And a voice from heaven said, "This is My beloved Son, in whom I am well pleased!"

Matthew 3:17

Psalm 2:7 You are My Son. This recalls 2 Sam. 7:8–16 as the basis for the Davidic king. It is the first OT reference to the Father/Son relationship—the paternal/filial roles—in the Trinity. Today I have begotten You. Rather than a reference to origin (there is no procreation within the Trinity), this vividly conveys the essential oneness shared between the Father and the Son. This verse is quoted in the NT with reference to the birth of Jesus (Heb. 1:5–6) and also to His resurrection (Acts 13:33–34) as the earthly affirmations. (2)

There is a cohesive thread throughout Scripture of the truth that Jesus is God's only begotten Son. Yes, we are adopted into God's family and are children of God (Galatians 4:5, Romans 8:15), but Jesus was born when the Spirit of God placed Him in Mary's womb supernaturally. The Trinity is a difficult concept, but the Bible teaches that the Son and the Father are One (John 10:30, John 17:22). In Hebrews 1, we read that Son is the exact representation of God's nature. The Holy Spirit is equated with God and the Son in Romans 8:9-11 and is the person of the Trinity that lives inside believers. You do not have to be able to completely wrap your mind around the concept of God and Jesus being One but also being Father and Son, to believe it. When the Father draws You or calls You to surrender your life to Jesus, He gives you the faith necessary to trust what the

Bible says about Him. Sometimes the best idea is follow Michael Card's advice in his song "To the Mystery" where he writes, "Give up on your pondering. Fall down on your knees!"

Father, we enjoy reading Your word and trusting the Holy Spirit to help us understand it but help us to always keep in mind that Your thoughts are higher than ours (Isaiah 55:9).

MESSIAH WILL BE BORN TO A VIRGIN

Therefore the Lord Himself will give you a sign: Behold, the virgin will be with child and will give birth to a son, and will call Him Immanuel.

Isaiah 7:14

So the angel told her, "Do not be afraid, Mary, for you have found favor with God. Behold, you will conceive and give birth to a son, and you are to give Him the name Jesus . . . "How can this be," Mary asked the angel, "since I am a virgin?"

Luke 1:30-31, 34

This is how the birth of Jesus Christ came about: His mother Mary was pledged in marriage to Joseph, but before they came together, she was found to be with child through the Holy Spirit. All this took place to fulfill what the Lord had said through the prophet: "Behold, the virgin will be with child and will give birth to a son, and they will call Him Immanuel" (which means, "God with us"). When Joseph woke up, he did as the angel of the Lord had commanded him, and embraced Mary as his wife. But he had no union with her until she gave birth to a Son. And he gave Him the name Jesus.

Matthew 1:18, 22-25

7:14 virgin. The Hebrew word occurs seven times in the Old Testament. It means a young woman of marriageable age, normally a virgin (Gen.

24:43). The Septuagint (the Greek translation of the Old Testament made about 150 b.c.) translated with a word more specifically meaning "virgin." The New Testament understands Isaiah to be designating the Virgin Mary (Matt. 1:23). (3)

Many biblical prophecies have both an imminent fulfillment and a distant future fulfillment. This may be the case with Isaiah 7:14. Several commentaries discussed the distinction between the Hebrew word used in Isaiah and another more specific Hebrew word for virgin. Since the word Isaiah used could be interpreted "young woman of marriageable age" or "virgin," it makes sense that the immediate fulfillment would be a young woman would give birth to a son named "God with Us" as a sign and encouragement to King Ahaz. Matthew and Luke both interpret Isaiah 7:14 as being fulfilled in their time by the virgin birth of Jesus, the Messiah. Matthew's target audience was primarily Jewish. Therefore, he often points out the prophecies fulfilled by Jesus to prove Him as Messiah. Susie dated a boy of Jewish heritage who had converted to Christianity. His mother had also received Christ and was so excited to read all the ways Jesus fulfilled the Old Testament prophecies concerning the Messiah. She was one of the most "on fire" Christians Susie knew at that time. She shared Jesus with every person God put in her path.

Our hope is that seeing the Old Testament prophecies paired with their New Testament fulfillments will strengthen your faith in Jesus as the Messiah—Christ or Anointed One. Share with us the awe of God's hand orchestrating His plan throughout history (HISstory)!

Father, we thank You for taking us on this journey through the Messianic prophecies!

Worship with Michael Card singing "Immanuel":
https://www.youtube.com/watch?v=O7DG3N6rYqk

MESSIAH: HE WILL BE CALLED BY GOD'S NAMES

For unto us a child is born, unto us a son is given, and the government will be upon His shoulders. And He will be called Wonderful Counselor, Mighty God, Everlasting Father, Prince of Peace. Of the increase of His government and peace there will be no end. He will reign on the throne of David and over his kingdom, to establish and sustain it with justice and righteousness from that time and forevermore. The zeal of the LORD of Hosts will accomplish this.

Isaiah 9:6-7

Therefore God exalted Him to the highest place and gave Him the name above all names, that at the name of Jesus every knee should bow, in heaven and on earth and under the earth, and every tongue confess that Jesus Christ is Lord, to the glory of God the Father.

Philippians 2:9-11

And this is His name by which He will be called: The LORD Our Righteousness.

Jeremiah 23:6b

A living gift—God's Messiah, the Hope of Israel, the long-awaited One entered our world as a tiny baby. His hair still wet from being born, He was already great, the greatest Gift ever bestowed upon humankind. This baby was born to be the King of kings and Lord of lords;

and in the future, He will reign over all the earth. He is already sovereign over everything, but not all people recognize that fact. In that day, when He returns to our world again, it will be obvious to all, and everyone will bow before Him. But even now, those who believe and trust in Him know Him by His many powerful names. Jesus is our Wonderful Counselor—One who listens and advises wisely to guide us through the maze of experiences to reach the Father. He is the Mighty God—He is equal with the Father and is our strength who enables us to stand firm as He holds us up. The Promised One is our Everlasting Father—His parenting is a forever commitment, and we are privileged to be His children. Jesus is ever-present and never-failing—He is always there for us, will never let us down, and will never disappoint. The Messiah is the Master of Wholeness, the Prince of Peace. The Hebrew word for peace, *shalom*—is synonymous with wholeness meaning "nothing missing, nothing broken." Jesus takes our broken pieces and makes us whole, enabling us to experience that true peace that passes all understanding (Philippians 4:6-7). Jesus is the Potter, and we are the clay. We are our Master's masterpiece: "But now, O LORD, You are our Father; we are the clay, and You are the potter; we are all the work of Your hand" (Isaiah 64:8)

Lord, of all Your names, our favorite is Everlasting Father. You are the Father who is always present, always faithful, and always loving us unconditionally. Thank You for adopting us into Your forever family!

"O Bethlehem[H1035] *Ephrathah, you are but a small Judean village, yet you will be the birthplace of my King who is alive from everlasting ages past!"*
Micah 5:2 (TLB)

Jesus answered, "I am the bread of life . . .
John 6:35a (BSB)

> H1035 *bayth leh'-khem*; from H1004 and H3899; house of bread; Beth-Lechem, a place in Palestine:—Bethlehem. (4)

TO BE BORN IN BETHLEHEM

People may have thought the King of all Israel
Would be born in the capital, Jerusalem.
But the prophet Micah had predicted
He'd be born in the village of Bethlehem.
Bethlehem was known as the hometown of David,
From whom the Messiah would descend.
David was a mighty king of Israel,
But the One to come would upend
Not only the Jews but every nation
For He was born to be King of kings.
The Magi from the East bowed in worship
And brought Him precious things.

For Jesus fulfilled this prophecy,
Born in tiny, obscure Bethlehem.
However, when He returns to this world
All people will bow low before Him;
For then it will be obvious
That He is the Lord of all.
Not only those who love Him
But evildoers before Him will fall.
The Baby laid in the manger
When there were no rooms to be found
Will return with the fanfare of trumpets
Which throughout the world will resound.
All those who refused to believe Him,
Will lie prostrate on their faces
And from their unwilling mouths
Will proclaim the King of king's praises.
Every knee shall bow, every tongue confess
That Jesus Christ is Lord—
That Baby born in Bethlehem
In fulfillment of God's word.

MESSIAH IS ETERNAL

But you, Bethlehem Ephrathah, who are small among the clans of Judah, out of you will come forth for Me One to be ruler over Israel—One whose origins are of old, from the days of eternity.

Micah 5:2

In the beginning was the Word, and the Word was with God, and the Word was God. He was with God in the beginning . . . The Word became flesh and made His dwelling among us. We have seen His glory, the glory of the one and only Son from the Father, full of grace and truth.

John 1:1-2, 14

Do not be afraid. I am the First and the Last, the Living One. I was dead, and behold, now I am alive forever and ever! And I hold the keys of Death and of Hades.

Revelation 1:17b-18

Micah prophesied that the Messiah would be eternal, existing before the creation of the world and yet to come as Israel's ruler. The Apostle John referred to Jesus as "the Word" and asserts that the Word not only was WITH God in the beginning but WAS God. In Revelation Jesus referred to Himself as the Alpha and Omega—the First and Last—the Living One. Jesus and God are One. Therefore, as God, Jesus has no beginning and no end. In the Gospel of John, Jesus made seven

"I AM" statements which Jewish listeners would understand as Him asserting His deity, the fact that He is God:

1. "I AM the Bread of Life" - John 6:35-48
2. "I AM the Light of the World" – John 8:12; 9:5
3. "I AM the Gate" – John 10:7
4. "I AM the Good Shepherd" – John 10:11-14
5. "I AM the Resurrection and the Life" – John 11:25
6. "I AM the Way, the Truth, and the Life" – John 14:6
7. "I AM the True Vine" – John 15:1-5

In John 14:9, Jesus told His disciples, "Anyone who has seen Me has seen the Father." As the incarnate God-man, Jesus began as a baby born of a virgin in Bethlehem and suffered the cruelest death of the time, crucifixion. However, His death on the earth was not an end but a beginning because on the third day, He rose from the dead and now continues His forever life seated at the right hand of God the Father. Jesus' resurrection completed His mission on earth, purchasing our redemption on the cross and paving the way for our resurrection into eternal life with Him by being the "firstborn of the dead" (Revelation 1:5). Since Christ was raised to life in bodily form, we, too, will be raised: "But Christ has indeed been raised from the dead, the firstfruits of those who have fallen asleep. . . But each in his own turn: Christ the firstfruits; then at His coming, those who belong to Him" (1 Corinthians 15:20 & 23).

Jesus is eternal and offers us eternal life with Him. If you have trusted Him, you will enjoy life with Him when your life here on earth ends or He returns. If you do not entrust your life to Him, you will still live forever; but that life will be one of separation from God and from everything that is good. Have you surrendered your life to Jesus, the One who died to redeem you from sin and death and rose again to prepare a place for those who belong to Him? If not, see "The Jewels of Salvation" toward the end of this book or please contact us for more information!
SRSlade2009@gmail.com or www.PreciousJewelsMinistries.com

Father, we thank You for making joyous, eternal life with You available to us through Jesus's incarnation, death, and resurrection from the grave! Thank You for drawing us and giving us the faith to entrust our lives to Christ.

Michael Card's "The Final Word": https://www.youtube.com/watch?v=U768-gCYods

BARREN NO MORE

But the angel said to him, "Do not be afraid, Zechariah, because your prayer has been heard. Your wife Elizabeth will bear you a son, and you are to give him the name John. He will be a joy and delight to you, and many will rejoice at his birth, for he will be great in the sight of the Lord. He shall never take wine or strong drink, and he will be filled with the Holy Spirit even from his mother's womb.

Luke 1:13-15

Think about the barren women in the Bible. Sarah conceived in her old age and gave birth to the child through whom all nations would be blessed. Rachel's sister outdid her in the giving birth category, but when the Lord opened Rachel's womb, he blessed her with Joseph who would save his people from famine. Hannah prayed for a son and promised to give him back to the Lord, and Samuel became the last judge and a prophet who would anoint Israel's first and second kings. God directed Samuel to choose David as Saul's successor. Ruth thought she might never have children, not due to her own barrenness, but because her husband died, leaving her childless. God provided the kinsman-redeemer Boaz, and she gave birth to the grandfather of King David. Elizabeth was barren, and like Sarah, was too old to conceive. However, the Lord opened her womb, and she gave birth to John the Baptist, the one who would prepare the way of the Lord, who while still in his mother's womb recognized the Messiah's mother and leapt for joy!

Perhaps you are feeling "barren," not literally but in your usefulness to the Lord. Keep praying. When He does give you a mission, obey Him, and be prepared for Him to do great things!

Father, we know that You can bless people with biological children miraculously or provide adopted children in unusual ways. You also give us spiritual children, the fruit of our testimonies and time spent discipling new believers. Lord, do not leave us barren in that second category, the spiritual children. Give us people to lead into Your Kingdom and nurture in Your ways.

MARY TO CARRY MESSIAH

So the angel told her, "Do not be afraid, Mary, for you have found favor with God. Behold, you will conceive and give birth to a son, and you are to give Him the name Jesus. He will be great and will be called the Son of the Most High. The Lord God will give Him the throne of His father David, and He will reign over the house of Jacob forever. His kingdom will never end!" "How can this be," Mary asked the angel, "since I am a virgin?" . . . "I am the Lord's servant," Mary answered. "May it happen to me according to your word." Then the angel left her.

Luke 1:30-34, 38

Let us set the scene: Mary was a young, devout, Jewish peasant girl going about her daily chores. She was pledged to marry a man named Joseph, but they were not even to the point of setting the wedding date. An angel suddenly appeared out of nowhere—not the norm in the obscure village of Nazareth or anywhere else for that matter. Mary shivered with fear because, in reality, angels are scary. The angel's opening line is that of most angels when they appear to mere humans, "Do not be afraid." Just when she is feeling a little bit better about the situation, he drops a bombshell on her. You're going to have a baby! And this is going to be no ordinary baby. Gabriel made it abundantly clear that she was to bear the Messiah. First, Mary was to name her baby "Jesus" meaning "Jehovah is generous. Jehovah saves." Then he said that Jesus would be called "Son of the Most High" meaning He would be God's Son as foretold in Psalm 2:7. He tops it off by declaring that her son would reign on David's throne forever and ever fulfilling the prophecies of Jeremiah 23:5 and Isaiah 9:6-7. If you read on a few verses in Luke chapter one, you will see that Mary was too overwhelmed to take all this in. She asked how this could happen since she was a virgin—a logical question from a human standpoint—but this was a mighty angel of God she was talking to. Gabriel patiently explained that God's Holy Spirit would accomplish placing the embryo in her womb and that with God nothing is impossible. Then in Luke 1:38, we have Mary's beautiful response to this unsettling announcement, "I am the Lord's servant," Mary answered. "May it happen to me according to your word."

God reveals His purposes for believers in His word, through godly preaching, and by the prompting of His Holy Spirit within. Mary was asked to risk her reputation and her relationship with Joseph and even give up her rights to her own body to carry God's Son in her womb. None of us will be asked to sacrifice in that exact same way. However, whatever God is calling us to do, we pray we will humbly reply, "May it happen to me according to your word." Mary did not achieve fame or fortune in her lifetime but has been remembered with reverence throughout history. We may receive no recognition for our obedience to God while we reside on this ball called earth. However, in Heaven, may we hear "Well done, good and faithful servant" (Matthew 25:21).

Father, we love and trust You. May Your will be done in our lives.

TENDER SURRENDER

The angel replied, "The Holy Spirit will come upon you, and the power of the Most High will overshadow you. So the Holy One to be born will be called the Son of God. Look, even Elizabeth your relative has conceived a son in her old age, and she who was called barren is in her sixth month. For no word from God will ever fail." "I am the Lord's servant," Mary answered. "May it happen to me according to your word." Then the angel left her.

Luke 1:35-38

Mary had been overwhelmed by the appearance of an angel. Her heart must have been pounding in her chest; she could probably hear it in her ears. She was probably filled with awe and wonder and some understandable fears. Would anyone believe her when she said she was pregnant with God's Son? Would Joseph stand by her side or assume the worst, that she had committed adultery? Would her fiancé have her stoned to death?! Who was she to raise the Son of the Most High? Would the Spirit that overcame her abide with her to guide her in raising God's child? As the thoughts raced through her mind, Mary became determined to accept this divine assignment and see it through. The angel had told her about Elizabeth's miracle and assured her that God's word to her would not fail. She had faith in Adonai (literally, My Lord) and would submit to all He asked of her. She would face the future with courage and grace.

She referred to herself as His servant, His handmaiden, His slave. In humility, she surrendered to God's will for her rather than running away.

Since we trust Jesus as our Savior and Lord, He may call us to unusual tasks. Surrender in humility to Him. Do whatever He asks. You may feel trepidation pounding in your chest, but His Spirit empowers you; for your Father always knows best. As God told Joshua, "Have I not commanded you to be strong and courageous? Do not be afraid; do not be discouraged, for the LORD your God is with you wherever you go" (Joshua 1:9).

Father, give us the courage to humbly surrender to Your will as Mary did so long ago. Help us to be Your handmaidens, but we thank You for elevating us to so much more, to be Your daughters!

Amy Grant singing "Breath of Heaven": https://www.youtube.com/watch?v=L8_475FKJWQ

When Elizabeth heard Mary's greeting, the baby leaped in her womb, and Elizabeth was filled with the Holy Spirit. In a loud voice she exclaimed, "Blessed are you among women, and blessed is the fruit of your womb! And why am I so honored, that the mother of my Lord should come to me? For as soon as the sound of your greeting reached my ears, the baby in my womb leaped for joy. Blessed is she who has believed that the Lord's word to her will be fulfilled."

Luke 1:41-45

Children are indeed a heritage from the LORD, and the fruit of the womb is His reward.

Psalm 127:3

JOHN JUMPS FOR JOY

Unborn baby in the womb,
at Mary's greeting, John jumped for joy.
Filled with the Spirit from conception,
he knew Messiah's mother's voice.
The Holy Spirit filled Elizabeth's heart
and enabled her to know
the presence of her Lord and Savior
in a holy Embryo.
Yet today's society justifies

the murder of an unborn baby,
debating when embryo becomes a person,
with no thought that maybe
since children are a gift from God
and the fruit of the womb a reward,
A fertilized egg, an embryo,
is declared a human soul by the Lord.
If you have already had an abortion,
you will find no judgment here.
Mary's baby was born to redeem you.
Forgiveness is yours! draw near
to Jesus who bore our sins on the cross,
the Lamb of God, our sacrifice.
Raised to life, He conquered the grave
and offers you paradise!

UNBORN BABY'S PRAISE

For as soon as the sound of your greeting reached my ears, the baby in my womb leaped for joy.
Luke 1:44

The exclamation in the scripture above was made by Elizabeth when her relative, Mary, came to visit her. Elizabeth was pregnant with the baby who would eventually become known as John the Baptist. The Holy Spirit revealed to fetus John that Mary was carrying the Messiah. Unborn John, utterly ecstatic, did gymnastics in his mother's womb. Elizabeth, also moved by the Holy Spirit, interpreted her baby's moves as leaping for joy. An UNBORN baby was the first to recognize our Savior, who was yet an EMBRYO. This is a strong argument for the fact that a fetus or even an embryo is already a person God has formed inside the mother-to-be. We are designed with purpose and intention from the beginning. In Psalm 139:13 (VOICE), the psalmist states, "For You shaped me, inside and out. You knitted me together in my mother's womb long before I took my first breath." Apparently, knitting is not just for "little old ladies." The Lord is a master knitter because He knit each of us together within our mother's wombs. That's a lot of knitting! God creates and knows intimately each embryo while still in the womb. God told Jeremiah, "Before I even formed you in your mother's womb, I knew all about you. Before you drew your first breath, I had already chosen you to be My prophet to speak My word to the nations" Jeremiah 1:4–5 (VOICE).

Before I was born, God created me for His purpose, to be His mouthpiece for His glory. He also knew I would face the daunting limitations of cerebral palsy. There are people who would have given up on a child with so many complexities. However, God placed many people in my life over the years to encourage me to be an overcomer rather than to wallow in self-pity. Knowing I would need a facilitator to accomplish my God-given purpose, the Lord formed Susie and used godly people to shape her into the person she is today. There are those who would end the life of an embryo, fetus, or even a baby thought to be less than "normal" before that child ever had an opportunity to live. Praise the Lord, He did not allow this to happen to me! God creates each one of us in the womb. That embryo, fetus, or baby is a person from the moment of conception, and to destroy that life is murder. One thing we must remember is that Jesus died to provide forgiveness for those who have made the choice to have an abortion. If you have had an abortion and you belong to Jesus, do not let Satan keep throwing that back at you. Memorize Romans 8:1, "Therefore, there is now no condemnation for those who are in Christ Jesus." You are forgiven. You are loved. You can be an instrument of God's grace to bless others. You are God's precious jewel!

An unborn fetus expressed exuberant joy due to the upcoming arrival of our Savior. How much more should we, who know the rest of the story, rejoice?

Father, we thank You for the gift of being born and even more so, for the gift of being born again by Your grace. We thank You that You designed us for a purpose and will enable us to fulfill that purpose in Your strength and for Your glory.

HUMBLE SERVANT MAGNIFIES THE LORD

Then Mary said: "My soul magnifies the Lord, and my spirit rejoices in God my Savior! For He has looked with favor on the humble state of His servant. From now on all generations will call me blessed.

Luke 1:46-48

Baby John was not the only one who was jumping for joy (Luke 1:41). Mary, under the influence of the Holy Spirit, burst into poetic song sometimes referred to as The Magnificat. Every fiber of Mary's being declared the greatness of her God who had transformed her into the mother of her own Savior. One of no special significance was carrying the One of supreme significance. John the Baptist would later declare, "He must increase, but I must decrease," (John 3:30); and Mary understood this concept well. She sang, not to draw attention to herself but to lift high the praises of God. She realized that God had chosen her, a humble but devout Jewish girl from a town known for no-goods. God chose a lowly peasant girl—probably a teenager—to be the mother of His only begotten Son because He was sending His Son to serve rather than to be served (Matthew 20:28). All generations have recognized the blessing God bestowed upon Mary, but those who read the gospels know that she endured much sorrow along with experiencing great joy. Mary is a prime example of how God chooses those who men would not necessarily choose. He chooses the weak to confound the mighty (1 Corinthians 1:27). Do not say to yourself that our omnipotent God cannot use you in mighty ways because you are weak, not very bright, too bad, or whatever excuse you come up with. None of us can have any worthwhile effect until we are in His hands, but the humblest life when fully committed and submitted to the Lord will be used to help turn the world upside down! (Acts 17:6)

Father, like Mary, we are amazed that You have chosen us, not only to be adopted into Your family but to have the privilege of speaking and teaching the truths found in Your word. Thank You for Your amazing grace!

Enjoy Mark Lowry, Guy Penrod, and David Phelps singing "Mary, Did You Know?": https://www.youtube.com/watch?v=3fbgWa5pH3g

But when the time had fully come, God sent His Son, born of a woman, born under the law, to redeem those under the law, that we might receive our adoption as sons.

Galatians 4:4-5

INCARNATION IN A NUTSHELL

The virgin Mary conceived God's Son
Angel told Joseph her baby's the One,
Messiah, Anointed,
By God appointed
Salvation for men with this Babe begun.

There were no rooms in Bethlehem
A stable was the best to be found for them
Mary gave birth
God came to earth
Shepherds came from the fields to worship Him.

The Baby Jesus was circumcised and redeemed
Simeon's eyes with tears of joy gleamed.
Simeon prophesied.
Anna evangelized.
The Spirit revealed this Babe was not as He seemed.

For this poor Baby Boy who had laid in a manger
Who had been King in Heaven was on earth a stranger.
Deity wrapped
in Baby who napped.
But soon His earthly life would be in danger.

Magi from the east entered Herod's court.
A strange phenomenon they had to report.
Glory shining as a star
Led the wise men from afar
to see a newborn King, so they came to consort.

Herod's advisors said Bethlehem was the place
Where their Messiah was foretold to show His face.
Wise men went
Where they were sent.
Meanwhile, Herod plotted to avoid being replaced.

The Magi found Mary in a house with the Babe
They opened their packs, and gifts they gave.
Gifts of great expense—
Gold, myrrh, frankincense.
They did not report to Herod, the Baby to save.

Joseph was warned by an angel to flee
To Egypt that night to protect his family.
Soldiers ravaged
As if they were savage
Killing all baby boys by King Herod's decree.

From the beginning, Satan tried to prevent
Jesus from the purpose of His advent.
Jesus survived
God kept Him alive
Until the time had come for which He was sent.

Jesus performed many miraculous signs,
Asserted His deity numerous ways and times
Sinners revealed
People were healed
When the timing was right, to Jerusalem He climbed.

There He was arrested, they yelled "Crucify."
The Babe in the manger had come here to die.
The perfect Lamb
The Great "I AM"
His mission on earth: to be our sacrifice.

He died on the cross, paid the ransom for sin
To redeem lost sinners who would trust in Him.
Three days in the tomb
Then life He resumed.
Arose to Father, promised we'll be with them.

Now Jesus is preparing a place for His bride
In His Father's abode, we will reside.
Jesus now intercedes
For His followers' needs
Until He returns and we walk by His side.

EMMANUEL (PART 1)

Therefore the Lord Himself will give you a sign: Behold, the virgin will be with child and will give birth to a son, and will call Him Immanuel[H6005].

Isaiah 7:14

H6005 im-maw-noo-ale' – A proper noun designating Immanuel, the name of the child who would serve as a sign to King Ahaz in his day and, in the fuller meaning of the prophecy, as a sign to the Lord's people Israel in the future. The name means "God with us". (5)

Emmanuel – I was about four or five years old, wearing my little leg braces, and I told my granddad, BJ Young, that I wanted Jesus to be mine forever and to be on His team. He carried me down to the altar to be led in prayer by Brother T. D. Hall, and that was it! I believe Jesus was, and is, and forever will be mine. (Susan)

Emmanuel – It was the summer before my sophomore year in high school when I realized that even though I was active in the youth group at my church, I did not have the relationship with God others had. I asked my youth minister, Ray Young, to talk with me; and he led me through the "Roman Road of Salvation". I prayed to receive God's free gift of grace, and immediately Jesus was with me. (Susie)

Emmanuel – At the age of 16, I had 200-300 stitches down my back after the surgeons corrected a 98° curvature of my spine to about 35°. I was in drastic pain, but Jesus was with me. In 2006, I was in the hospital awaiting a lithotripsy to blast kidney stones. My surgeon felt an urgency to check on me and found me unresponsive and not breathing. While I was on the ventilator for three weeks, God was with me and specifically told me to minister to His shepherds. When both of my legs had to be amputated above the knee, I coded again. Once again, the presence of the Lord sustained me. (Susan)

Emmanuel – When my husband left me five days before our first wedding anniversary, I yelled at God; but God was with me and led me that Sunday (our first anniversary) to a church family that saw me through my divorce and discipled me to walk more closely with the Lord. When my daddy went to be with the Lord after a battle with cancer, I found I could "dance like a child" in God's presence even though my heart was breaking. As I cared for my mother for six years, Jesus was with us every step of the way. (Susie)

EMMANUEL (Part 2)

This is how the birth of Jesus Christ came about: His mother Mary was pledged in marriage to Joseph, but before they came together, she was found to be with child through the Holy Spirit. Because Joseph her husband was a righteous man and was unwilling to disgrace her publicly, he resolved to divorce her quietly. But after he had pondered these things, an angel of the Lord appeared to him in a dream and said, "Joseph, son of David, do not be afraid to embrace Mary as your wife, for the One conceived in her is from the Holy Spirit. She will give birth to a Son, and you are to give Him the name Jesus, because He will save His people from their sins." All this took place to fulfill what the Lord had said through the prophet: "Behold, the virgin will be with child and will give birth to a son, and they will call Him Emmanuel" ^{G1694} *(which means, "God with us").*
Matthew 1:18-23

> G1694 em-man-oo-ale'; of Hebrew origin (H6005); God with us; Emmanuel, a name of Christ:—Emmanuel. (6)

Emmanuel – When I graduated from ORU with my bachelor's and then master's degrees and later, when I was ordained as a minister, God was with me. When I celebrated entering my "golden decade" even though my life expectancy had been 24 years, Jesus celebrated the continued life He gives me. Jesus has been with me mightily through every high and low in my life. I trust that He will continue to be my Emmanuel, God with me, until He receives me home. My desire is to be a living gift of His presence to those I encounter. (Susan)

Emmanuel – When the Lord blessed me with "adopted" teenagers in my forties, I knew Jesus was with me and was giving me the children I always prayed and believed He would. God has given me many Christian friends who are "Jesus with skin on" and through them, He has hugged me so many times. Jesus brought Susan and me together and has enabled us by His grace to form Precious Jewels Ministries, and we are keenly aware of Emmanuel, God with us, every day as we study His word. (Susie)

Emmanuel – Take a few moments to really contemplate how Jesus is "God with us" in your own life. Maybe even write examples as we each did. Praise and thank Him for His presence!

Emmanuel, Jesus, thank You for being God with us! May we continue to celebrate and bask in Your presence daily, and may our lives bring glory to Your name—Emmanuel.

Enjoy "God with Us" by Mercy Me: https://www.youtube.com/watch?v=o5Y-Px39cm4

WHAT'S IN A NAME?

She will give birth to a Son, and you shall name Him Jesus (The Lord is salvation), for He will save His people from their sins."
Matthew 1:21 (AMP)

She will bear a Son, and you shall call His name Jesus [the Greek form of the Hebrew Joshua, which means Savior], for He will save His people from their sins [that is, prevent them from failing and missing the true end and scope of life, which is God].
Matthew 1:21 (AMPC)

She will give birth to a son, and you are to name him Yeshua, [which means 'Adonai saves,'] because he will save his people from their sins."
Matthew 1:21 (CJB)

When the angel appeared to Joseph to assure him that Mary had not been unfaithful and explain that her baby was God's Son, he instructed Joseph to name the baby "Jesus." One must understand that in their culture most firstborn boys were named after their father which mean Jesus would have logically been named Joseph. Why the name Jesus? The translations of Matthew 1:21 above reveal the answer. He was named according to His God-given purpose to be the Savior of all who would put their trust in Him. Jesus (Yeshua or Joshua) means "Adonai saves." Who is Adonai? Adonai is a word used by the Hebrews for God meaning "my Lord." It derives from a word that can mean "master" or "sovereign." Therefore, the name Jesus means "the sovereign Lord God saves." God did not have to send Jesus in the form of a baby to grow into the perfect God-Man and die on the cross to provide redemption from our sin. In His sovereign grace, He chose to do so out of His love for His people. The name Jesus should be precious on our lips. Even His name, when properly understood, proclaims the Good News that through Him salvation is made available to those who believe. His name indicates a sovereign Lord who was willing, ready, and able to redeem His chosen ones from sin and death. May we be sure to revere His name. May we never use it in vain, flippantly, or as a curse word. May we speak it tenderly in thanksgiving and cry out in His name in times of trouble. May we remember that He is our Master and Sovereign who loves us with everlasting love. As the Gaithers sing, "Jesus, Jesus, Jesus, There's just something about that name . . ."

Father, we thank You for Jesus, Your perfect, sinless, Passover Lamb, who sacrificed Himself in our place on the cross. We thank You that when we whisper the name "Jesus," You are right here as our Emmanuel, God with us!

Worship with the Gaithers singing "There's Something About That Name" https://www.youtube.com/watch?v=x4KwBkajCzs

So Joseph also went up from Nazareth in Galilee to Judea, to the city of David called Bethlehem, since he was from the house and line of David. He went there to register with Mary, who was pledged to him in marriage and was expecting a child. While they were there, the time came for her Child to be born. And she gave birth to her firstborn, a Son. She wrapped Him in swaddling cloths and laid Him in a manger, because there was no room for them in the inn.

Luke 2:4-7

AS A BABY, HE CAME

A long time ago in Bethlehem
a tiny Babe was born,
The King of kings and Lord of lords
on earth in mortal form.
What did it mean for Christ to come
to walk on earth as man?
And what is the significance
of this part of God's plan?
I've often thought it interesting
that Christ came as a child,
A little, tiny baby,
helpless, meek, and mild.

But since He came in just that way,
I know He understands
Every small frustration
of living as a man.
He understands the growing pains
of our own little ones,
Although when He was twelve years old,
He knew He was God's Son.
He knows just how it feels
to go through difficult teen years.
He knows the loss of friends through death.
He knew pain, and He cried tears.
My Jesus knew temptation
and yet remained sin-free.
He was the perfect sacrifice
who died for you and me.
So, we celebrate each year
the coming of our King.
Because He came with love for us,
His praises we joyfully sing.

SHEPHERDS SHAKING IN THEIR SANDALS

And there were shepherds residing in the fields nearby, keeping watch over their flocks by night. Just then an angel of the Lord stood before them, and the glory of the Lord shone around them, and they were terrified. But the angel said to them, "Do not be afraid! For behold, I bring you good news of great joy that will be for all the people: Today in the city of David a Savior has been born to you. He is Christ the Lord! And this will be a sign to you: You will find a baby wrapped in swaddling cloths and lying in a manger."

Luke 2:8-12

> Shepherds were a despised class because their work prevented them from keeping the ceremonial law, and as they moved about the country it was common for them to be regarded as thieves. They were considered unreliable and were not allowed to give evidence in the courts. (7)

Shepherds were on one of the lowest rungs of society's ladder. That God chose to announce the birth of His Son first to this group of people is evidence that He shows no partiality of class. His interest is solely in the hearts of humanity, not where they are on the socio-economic strata. He invited the shepherds who may have been tending the sacrificial lambs to be the first to worship the perfect Lamb of God. They were allowed VIP access even before the Magi, the wise men, from the east. The shepherds were terrified or as the KJV puts it "sore afraid." The shepherds were shaking in their sandals! Imagine how you would respond if you were out in the middle of nowhere on a pitch-black night, and suddenly the sky lit up like daylight! When angels appear, the first response is to fall on your face afraid. Angels almost always begin with "Fear not!" because their appearance can be overwhelming. There are 365 "fear nots" in the Bible—one for each day of the year. (Stop and think about that!) This angel declared he had something good to tell them—joyful news of the Messiah's birth. The fact that the angels said the good news was for ALL people would be most important to these shepherds who were considered second-class citizens. They were viewed almost as the homeless are today—dirty, unworthy, and possibly criminals. The Angel used three names to describe the baby: Savior (Liberator), Christ or Messiah (Anointed One), and Lord (Supreme Authority). The amazing thing to these men was that He was born for them! He was the Messiah of the underdog as well as the top dog! To their astonishment, they were told that this Baby King was born in a stable and would actually be lying where the cattle fed! The shepherds themselves had probably been born somewhere better than a stable!

The Lord invited the lowliest people, shepherds, to be the first to see the baby Jesus. In the same way, He first appeared to women (another group who could not testify in court) after His resurrection. Never think of yourself as below God's notice. Jesus esteems people very differently than our society.

Father, thank You that "While we were still sinners, Christ died for us" (Romans 5:8b)!

REJOICE! THE REDEEMER IS FINALLY HERE

But the angel said to them, "Do not be afraid! For behold, I bring you good news of great joy that will be for all the people: Today in the city of David a Savior has been born to you. He is Christ the Lord! And this will be a sign to you: You will find a baby wrapped in swaddling cloths and lying in a manger."

Luke 2:10-12

The great joy the angels proclaimed was not to be for the Jews only but for all nations, all those who come to know Jesus. Repeatedly, the news of Jesus' birth is declared to be a joyous occasion. The long-awaited Messiah, the Redeemer, had arrived and would eventually offer Himself up as a sacrifice to rescue those who trust in Him from suffering the wrath of God and the penalty of their sins. Israel, a nation conquered by Rome, had been plunged into deep darkness. Jesus was not the military conqueror whom they were expecting and for whom they hoped. However, He freed them from the greater captivity of sin, bringing those who believe an overwhelming peace and everlasting joy. They were looking for Jesus to be a conqueror and set up a powerful kingdom, to lead them into battle, and to overthrow Rome. However, He came as a Lamb led silently to slaughter (Isaiah 53:7). The Law God gave to Moses required that lambs with no blemish or spot be sacrificed to Him to atone for the people's sins. John the Baptist declared, "Look, the Lamb of God, who takes away the sin of the world!" (John 1:29b). Jesus, the final perfect Passover Lamb, chose to die on the cross in our place to pay for our sins. He rose again to bring all those who trust and believe in Him into the perfect kingdom of love and peace.

I realized the truth that Jesus died for me at a very early age. I was about four or five years old, sitting in church with my granddad. The pastor was still preaching about our need to be on the right team when I told my granddad that I wanted to go. I didn't want to be separated from Jesus. I wanted to be on His team and live with Him forever someday in heaven. So, my granddad took me up in his arms and carried me, heavy metal and leather leg braces and all, to the altar even before the sermon ended! I told the preacher, Brother T.D. Hall, "I want to receive Jesus into my heart. I want to live with Him and not be His enemy." From that day forward, the Holy Spirit has lived in me. I am a citizen of His kingdom even while I am still in this earth-suit. Though I am not yet healed physically, I have been healed in the most important way: I have been delivered from my sin and am being transformed into the likeness of Christ! Someday, I will live with Him in the forever home He has prepared for all those who love Him. If you have trusted Jesus as your Savior, He has brought you into His kingdom, too. Rejoice!!!

Philippians 3:20-21 But our citizenship is in heaven,

and we eagerly await a Savior from there, the Lord Jesus Christ, who, by the power that enables Him to subject all things to Himself, will transform our lowly bodies to be like His glorious body.

Father, thank You for sending Jesus to redeem us and set us free from the slavery of sin. Thank You for His promise to prepare a place for us and return to take us into His home.

"Celebrate the Child" with Michael Card: https://www.youtube.com/watch?v=jXGiYOIJtec
Listen to "Scandalon" also by Michael Card: https://www.youtube.com/watch?v=6Vj6Rv5WvIo

SHEPHERDS SEEK SWADDLED SAVIOR

When the angels had left them and gone into heaven, the shepherds said to one another, "Let us go to Bethlehem and see this thing that has happened, which the Lord has made known to us." So they hurried off and found Mary and Joseph and the Baby, who was lying in the manger.

Luke 2:15-16

The shepherds immediately set off on a journey to seek this Baby Savior. The angel had told them the baby would be wrapped in "swaddling cloths" and lying in a manger. Research revealed many things we did not previously know about "swaddling cloths."

1. Swaddling cloths could also be used as burial clothes   http://living4jesus.net/dynamic/in.swaddling.htm

2. It was the custom in the Middle East to wash the newborn baby in salted water and wrap them in swaddling cloths. Artist Jenedy Paige's painting "Little Lamb" depicts Jesus in a stone manger resembling a stone altar, wrapped in cloths with symbols of Mary and Joseph's lineage embroidered on them. She explains that when a woman married, she lovingly embroidered these strips of cloth. These were the linen strips wrapped around the couple's hands in their marriage ceremony and later

clothed their newborn wrapping the child in a symbol of his/her parents' covenant commitment.

See an interview with Jenedy Paige here: https://www.youtube.com/watch?v=0fAkq75B6nY

3. We read that the shepherds to whom the angels appeared were keeping watch over the lambs to be used for Passover sacrifices. When an ewe was ready to deliver, the shepherds would take her into a cave and wrap the newborn lamb in swaddling clothes to prevent it from injury and deformity because the sacrifice had to be perfect. https://sites.google.com/site/beautifulbiblefacts/lamb-in-swaddling-cloths-lying-in-a-manger

These shepherds would understand the concept of swaddling God's perfect Lamb. Many years later, some of them might have recalled seeing the newborn Messiah who became the perfect sacrifice for their sins wrapped in swaddling clothes like a sacrificial lamb. The stone manger/altar, the swaddling/burial cloths, and later the myrrh brought by Magi—a spice used in burial—all foreshadowed the Baby's ultimate purpose for becoming a man. Jesus came to this earth, ultimately, to be God's final, perfect Lamb sacrificed to redeem us from sin.

As you celebrate the Baby Jesus in the manger this year, remember that He was literally "born to die" for YOU! Worship Him as Savior and Lord!

Father, the shepherds rushed into the night to seek Jesus. Help us to be that eager to know more of Him! We

"want to know Christ and the power of His resurrection and the fellowship of His sufferings, being conformed to Him in His death" (Philippians 3:10).

Worship with Michael Card singing "To the Mystery": https://www.youtube.com/watch?v=KkVmo7op-o8

SHEPHERDS HERALD THE GOOD SHEPHERD'S ARRIVAL

When the angels had left them and gone into heaven, the shepherds said to one another, "Let us go to Bethlehem and see this thing that has happened, which the Lord has made known to us." So they hurried off and found Mary and Joseph and the Baby, who was lying in the manger. After they had seen the Child, they spread the message they had received about Him. And all who heard it were amazed at what the shepherds said to them. But Mary treasured up all these things and pondered them in her heart. The shepherds returned, glorifying and praising God for all they had heard and seen, which was just as the angel had told them.

Luke 2:15-20

I am the good shepherd. The good shepherd lays down His life for the sheep.

John 10:11

An angel appeared to a group of mere shepherds and made the astonishing announcement that the Messiah had been born in Bethlehem. He gave them the even more surprising news that this Holy Baby would be found sleeping in a feeding trough for animals! Then as quickly as the host of angels had appeared in glorious light, they vanished, and the shepherds were once again alone in the dark. The shepherds, like excited children on Christmas morning, ran to see God's gift to the world. They found everything exactly like the angel had said. Afterward, they did the same thing we did as children—they told the entire neighborhood about the best gift they had received—a baby born to be the Messiah. They reluctantly went back to the drudgery of guarding their sheep but with a newfound awe of the Lord. They praised and glorified God as they returned. We wonder if the sheep could sense the change in their shepherds or if even they were aware that the best Shepherd of all was now living among men? Just as we share about our "best Christmas ever," we are certain those shepherds passed down the story of the night they found their Savior lying in a manger. We imagine their children and grandchildren, eyes bright with wonder, saying, "Tell it again! Tell about the angels and the Baby!" May the wide-eyed wonder of the Christmas story fill our hearts throughout the Year! May the Spirit of Christmas, the celebration of God's perfect Gift, permeate our lives every day! And may we, like the shepherds, share the Good News everywhere we go about the Savior born in Bethlehem!

Father, let us see once again with wide-eyed wonder the Baby in the manger who was born to die in our place. May the miracle of the virgin birth and even more-so, the miracle of the resurrection constantly fill us with joy! And may we, like the shepherds long ago, proclaim the Messiah to everyone we meet and give the gift of true hope this Christmas!

Zach Williams "Go Tell it on the Mountain": https://www.youtube.com/watch?v=mXBzrutelZA

When the eight days until His circumcision had passed, He was named Jesus, the name the angel had given Him before He had been conceived. And when the time of purification according to the Law of Moses was complete, His parents brought Him to Jerusalem to present Him to the Lord (as it is written in the Law of the Lord: "Every firstborn male shall be consecrated to the Lord"), and to offer the sacrifice specified in the Law of the Lord: "A pair of turtledoves or two young pigeons."

Luke 2:21-24

But if she cannot afford a lamb, she shall bring two turtledoves or two young pigeons, one for a burnt offering and the other for a sin offering. Then the priest will make atonement for her, and she will be clean.

Leviticus 12:8

The sum to be paid for redeeming anyone a month old or over is to be five shekels of silver (two ounces), as you value it, using the sanctuary shekel (this is the same as twenty gerahs).

Numbers 18:16 (CJB)

But when the time had fully come, God sent His Son, born of a woman, born under the law, to redeem those under the law, that we might receive our adoption as sons.

Galatians 4:4-5

REDEEMER REDEEMED

The Baby lovingly placed in a stone manger
Would someday die on a cross made of wood.
Jesus was born to be our Redeemer
Which meant He must do everything as He should.
In order to be the spotless Lamb of God,
He must obey every point of the Law.
So, Mary and Joseph brought five shekels of silver
To redeem the Baby they had laid on the straw.
Our Redeemer as firstborn had to be redeemed
and his mother purified by offering two doves.
Mary could not even afford a spotless lamb
When presenting the Lamb of our Father's love.
The parents God chose to raise His Son
Fulfilled all that the Law demanded.
Mary and Joseph obeyed Gabriel's message,
Doing everything the Lord commanded.

REDEEMING THE LONG-AWAITED REDEEMER

When the eight days until His circumcision had passed, He was named Jesus, the name the angel had given Him before He had been conceived. And when the time of purification according to the Law of Moses was complete, His parents brought Him to Jerusalem to present Him to the Lord (as it is written in the Law of the Lord: "Every firstborn male shall be consecrated to the Lord"), and to offer the sacrifice specified in the Law of the Lord: "A pair of turtledoves or two young pigeons."

Luke 2:21-24

When Pharaoh was unwilling to let us go, Adonai killed all the firstborn males in the land of Egypt, both the firstborn of humans and the firstborn of animals. This is why I sacrifice to Adonai any male that is first from the womb of an animal, but all the firstborn of my sons I redeem.

Exodus 13:15 (CJB)

The sum to be paid for redeeming anyone a month old or over is to be five shekels of silver (two ounces), as you value it, using the sanctuary shekel (this is the same as twenty gerahs).

Numbers 18:16 (CJB)

Abraham was given instructions concerning circumcision of baby boys who were eight days old as a sign of the covenant between the Lord and His people (Genesis 17:9-14). Therefore, Jesus was circumcised as the Law required on the eighth day. In the Bible, numbers have meaning. Eight is the number of new beginnings, and Jesus came to bring us the New Covenant. In obedience to what the angel had told both Mary and Joseph, they named Him Jesus which means "Adonai is generous, Adonai saves." God's free gift of grace was extravagantly purchased by Jesus on the cross to save us from our sins, a generous gift indeed. Before Jesus created the world, before He spoke everything into being, He was "...the Lamb slain from the foundation of the world" Revelation 13:8b (KJV). This means that even before Adam and Eve could sin and be deceived, God in His mercy, had cleaned up the mess of sin, and would reveal this message at the perfect moment in time. In God's accounting of time, it was as if Jesus had already gone to the cross. After Mary waited the required 40 days for purification, Mary and Joseph took the Baby to the Temple in Jerusalem. As the firstborn male, He was to be dedicated to God as a priest or redeemed by paying five shekels. Two turtledoves or two young pigeons was the sacrifice for purification for a mother after birth for poor people who did not own or have the ability to purchase a perfect lamb (Leviticus 12:1-8) However, they were dedicating THE PERFECT LAMB! Mary and Joseph were devout Jews following all the Law prescribed concerning the Baby Jesus and Mary's purification after childbirth. Jesus placed Himself under the Law from the moment of His birth.

Galatians 4:4-5 (NIV): But when the set time had fully come, God sent his Son, born of a woman, born under the law, to redeem those under the law, that we might receive adoption to sonship.

Ponder This: Jesus, who was God in the flesh, placed Himself under the law. He was the only man who perfectly obeyed the law, remaining sinless. He who gave the Law to Moses, subjected Himself to it in order to free us from the burden it placed upon humankind. Even as a baby, Jesus had to be redeemed as all firstborn children belonged to God. Imagine—the Redeemer had to be redeemed!

Father, thank You for sending Your Son to redeem us!

Simeon took Him in his arms and blessed God, saying: "Sovereign Lord, as You have promised, You now dismiss Your servant in peace. For my eyes have seen Your salvation, which You have prepared in the sight of all people, a light for revelation to the Gentiles, and for glory to Your people Israel."

Luke 2:28-32

In Him was life, and that life was the light of men. The Light shines in the darkness, and the darkness has not overcome it.

John 1:4-5

THE LIGHT

Simeon had waited a lifetime
To see the Messiah with his own eyes.
The Lord had told him this would happen
Before the day that he died.
The Spirit led him into the temple
At the precise time of the day
That His parents were redeeming
The Babe who had laid on the hay.
Simeon recognized his Savior
And his heart was filled with joy.

He immediately sang prophecy
Concerning this baby Boy.
This Child would bring glory to Israel
But was not for the Jews alone.
He was the Light to guide the Gentiles,
And for all believers' sins to atone.
The star that would guide the Magi
Would continue to shine through the Christ.
He would die on a cross to redeem us,
But nothing could hold back His life.
Since the Father resurrected Jesus,
We, like Simeon, can have complete peace;
For His Light that shines in the darkness
Assures us of joy that will never cease.

There was also a prophetess named Anna, the daughter of Phanuel, of the tribe of Asher, who was well along in years. She had been married for seven years, and then was a widow to the age of eighty-four. She never left the temple, but worshiped night and day, fasting and praying. Coming forward at that moment, she gave thanks to God and spoke about the Child to all who were waiting for the redemption of Jerusalem.

Luke 2:36-38

ANNA: INTERCESSOR, PROPHETESS, EVANGELIST

Anna was a widow
who worshipped God every day,
dedicating her life
to honor Him and pray.
She saw the Baby Jesus
and knew He was the One
promised to Israel,
God's only begotten Son.
She offered thanks
and not only praised
but spread news of the Christ
the rest of her days.

Intercessor, prophetess,
and evangelist was she.
When we are over eighty,
in God's service, we will be.

Star Gazers

When they saw the star, they rejoiced with great delight.
Matthew 2:10

The magi (wise men) had seen a great star from their country in the east and had read a prophecy of a king to be born of the Jews. They had set out following the star, but it disappeared for a time. They inquired of the Jews' current king, Herod, where this child was to be born. After his scholars informed them the child was to be born in Bethlehem, they set back out on their journey, and the star reappeared. The wise men were not just full of joy when the star came back into view: their joy was exponentially overwhelming. It was also a relief that they could now fulfill their hearts' desire to worship the baby King. They may or may not have understood that the God of the universe was Jesus' Father, but they saw the celestial birthday candle, the ultimate celebratory sign in the heavens, to celebrate the birth of His chosen One. The star, which may have even been the Shekhinah glory of God, led them to the house where Jesus and His earthly parents were staying, and they worshipped Him and gave Him gifts.

Think for just a moment of the glory Jesus left behind in Heaven to endure a humble birth in a stable, being subject to earthly parents, living under the limitations of being a man, and ultimately the sacrifice and humiliation of the cross in order to redeem His forever family. Sometimes the Lord leads us to travel along a difficult path. However, we will never face a journey as difficult as His incarnation and life among humankind. When you begin to feel that your burdens seem to outweigh your blessings, remember what Jesus suffered for you. Remember that our trials here are but a breath compared to the everlasting glory we will experience because we have surrendered our lives to Jesus. "For our light and momentary affliction is producing for us an eternal weight of glory that is far beyond comparison" 2 Corinthians 4:17. The CNA (Certified Nurse Assistant) who helped Susie care for her mom always told her, "Whatever the Lord calls you to suffer, He will enable you to endure." Even more than that, we know that we will come out victorious! "No, in all these things we are more than conquerors through Him who loved us" Romans 8:37.

Father, the wise men left their home in the East and traveled a great distance to bring gifts to the Baby King of Israel, Jesus. Lord, help us to follow Your Light wherever You lead us. Help us to constantly seek Your kingdom above all else and trust You to provide our needs (Matthew 6:33). As we seek to follow Your Light, help us to rejoice with great joy like the wise men did so long ago.

Worship with Gaither family of musicians featuring The Martins singing "Rejoice With Exceeding Great Joy:" https://www.youtube.com/watch?v=cYRrHGE9QJo

Worship with Larry Ford singing "Follow Me:" https://www.youtube.com/watch?v=RN8UW_C_sgA

HE SHALL BE CALLED A NAZARENE

And he came and dwelt in a city called Nazareth: That it might be fulfilled which was spoken by the prophets, He shall be called a Nazarene.

Matthew 2:23

"Can anything good come from Nazareth?" Nathanael asked. "Come and see," said Philip.

John 1:46

2:23 "He shall be called a Nazarene." Nazareth, an obscure town 70 mi. N of Jerusalem, was a place of lowly reputation, and nowhere mentioned in the OT. Some have suggested that "Nazarene" is a reference to the Heb. word for branch in Is. 11:1. Others point out that Matthew's statement that "prophets" had made this prediction may be a reference to verbal prophecies nowhere recorded in the OT. A still more likely explanation is that Matthew is using "Nazarene" as a synonym for someone who is despised or detestable—for that was how people from the region were often characterized (cf. John 1:46). If that is the case, the prophecies Matthew has in mind would include Ps. 22:6–8; Is. 49:7; 53:3. (8)

When the Lord told Joseph and Mary to come back from Egypt where they had fled due to Herod's plan to murder all the boys up to two years of age in Bethlehem, they set their course for the town where they had met and married—Nazareth. Matthew's gospel notes that prophets had foretold that the Messiah would be called a Nazarene. By the time of Jesus, Nazarene was synonymous with despised or detestable. Apparently, the people from that city had a horrible reputation. This is why Nathanael questioned whether the Messiah could truly be from Nazareth. Jesus was so identified with Nazareth that people did not realize He was born in Bethlehem as evidenced in chapter seven of John's gospel.

John 7:41-42 Others declared, "This is the Christ." But still others asked, "How can the Christ come from Galilee? Doesn't the Scripture say that the Christ will come from the line of David and from Bethlehem, the village where David lived?"

Have you ever experienced discrimination because of the place you grew up or currently live? Or perhaps due to your ethnicity or color? Or in Susan's case, her cerebral palsied earth-suit? Our Lord experienced discrimination as well. The word tells us that God doesn't look at those things about us. Passages such as James 2, Romans 12:9-21, and 1 Peter chapter 3 speak about God's impartiality and how we are to treat one another with non-judgmental love. Avoid discriminating against others by remembering how God looks at them and at you: "God sees not as man sees, for man looks at the outward appearance, but the Lord looks at the heart" (1 Samuel 16:7b NASB).

Father, help us see others with Your eyes of love and compassion. Give us the discernment to see past the outward shell and get to know the hearts of people.

Therefore He is able to save completely those who draw near to God through Him, since He always lives to intercede for them.

Hebrews 7:25

CHRISTMAS CONTEMPLATION

Eternal Father, strong to save
We marvel at the gift You gave,
Implanting Your Son in a virgin's womb
Knowing He would face death and the tomb.

His mother's heart would someday grieve.
His brothers would be slow to believe.
They thought Him crazy and stated so,
But after He rose, then they would know.

Teaching, healing He came to serve
even those who did not deserve
The Sacrifice He came to be—
Guilty ones like you and me.

Ungrateful people with blinded eyes
Willfully failed to recognize
God incarnate, not mere man,
Fulfillment of Your perfect plan.

Our great High Priest, He entered in
Where no high priest had ever been
In the very presence of the Holy One
By sacrificing Himself, God's only Son.

Now seated at the King's right hand,
He ever lives to intercede for man.
The only mediator we need
Was Jesus who was born to bleed.

Oh, gracious Father, kind and true,
May we forever worship You.
As we celebrate our dear Lord's birth,
Remind us why He walked on earth.

For unto us a child is born, unto us a son is given, and the government will be upon His shoulders. And He will be called Wonderful Counselor, Mighty God, Everlasting Father, Prince of Peace. Of the increase of His government and peace there will be no end. He will reign on the throne of David and over his kingdom, to establish and sustain it with justice and righteousness from that time and forevermore. The zeal of the LORD of Hosts will accomplish this.

Isaiah 9:6-7

CHRISTMAS

Christ's incarnation and crucifixion:
    planned before creation.
He would be the Seed of Eve,
    born to stomp the serpent's head.
Rising, bright Star of Jacob,
    son of Isaac, son of Abraham
In Judah's line by Tamar,
    Jesus would be the Lion of Praise.
Son of David, heir to an everlasting throne,
    Son of the Most High
To be born in Bethlehem, Bread of Life
    born in "House of Bread"
Messiah was born to a virgin and called
    Emanuel—God with us
Above all names the Name of Jesus,
    Mighty God, Prince of Peace
Savior, Creator, Wonderful Counselor,
    Everlasting Father,

JESUS!

JEWELS OF SALVATION

❖ *Romans 3:22-24 And this righteousness from God comes through faith in Jesus Christ to all who believe. There is no distinction, **for all have sinned and fall short of the glory of God** and are justified freely by His grace through the redemption that is in Christ Jesus.*

Everyone on earth has sinned. Sin is both doing things that go against what God tells us to do in the Bible and failing to do the good things He instructs us to do. This failure brings the wrath of God on us, and Jesus is the **only way** to make peace with God. John 14:6 "Jesus answered, 'I am the way and the truth and the life. No one comes to the Father except through Me.'"

❖ *Romans 6:20-23 For when you were slaves to sin, you were free of obligation to righteousness. What fruit did you reap at that time from the things of which you are now ashamed? The outcome of those things is death. But now that you have been set free from sin and have become slaves to God, the fruit you reap leads to holiness, and the outcome is eternal life. **For the wages of sin is death, but the gift of God is eternal life in Christ Jesus our Lord.***

The punishment for sin is death. The official term is "substitutionary atonement" which simply means you were sentenced to the death penalty, but Jesus volunteered to die on the cross in your place in order for you to be set free. Jesus died a painful death to redeem you from slavery to sin and spare you from the wrath of the righteous, Holy God.

❖ *Romans 5:6-8 For at just the right time, while we were still powerless, Christ died for the ungodly. Very rarely will anyone die for a righteous man, though for a good man someone might possibly dare to die.* ***But God proves His love for us in this: While we were still sinners, Christ died for us.***

Jesus died while we were still sinners. "For God so loved the world that **He gave His one and only Son**, that everyone who believes in Him shall not perish but have eternal life." John 3:16.

❖ *Romans 10:8-10 But what does it say? "The word is near you; it is in your mouth and in your heart," that is, the word of faith we are proclaiming: that **if you confess with your mouth, "Jesus is Lord," and believe in your heart that God raised Him from the dead, you will be saved.** For with your heart you believe and are justified, and with your mouth you confess and are saved.*
1 Corinthians 15:3-4 "For what I received I passed

on to you as of first importance: that Christ died for our sins according to the Scriptures, that He was buried, that He was raised on the third day according to the Scriptures . . ." If you believe that Jesus is the Son of God who died for you and was raised to life, then trust in—rely on—Him to save you from the wrath of God, you can belong to Jesus.

❖ *Romans 10:11-13 It is just as the Scripture says: "Anyone who believes in Him will never be put to shame." For there is no difference between Jew and Greek: The same Lord is Lord of all, and gives richly to all who call on Him, for,* **"Everyone who calls on the name of the Lord will be saved."**

How do you become a member of the family of God? Pray—talk to God admitting that you cannot be good enough because you could *never* perfectly obey all His commands. Tell Him you trust that Jesus died on the cross to save you from slavery to sin and the wrath of God. Ask God to place His Holy Spirit in you and change you from the inside out. Thank Him for giving you life in His presence forever.

BELIEVER'S BENEFITS

The obvious benefit of trusting in Jesus, the Son of God who died for you and was raised from the grave to return to the right hand of His Father, and surrendering your life to him, is that instead of spending eternity separated from God and all that is good you will live in His presence in complete peace and joy. However, those who become the Lord's children by relying on Jesus gain many other things in this current life on earth. Here are a few:

❖ Lord, we thank you for freeing us from slavery to sin and providing a way to flee temptation! Romans 6:6 "We know that our old self was crucified with Him so that the body of sin might be rendered powerless, that we should no longer be slaves to sin." This does not mean that a believer will never sin again. It means he/she now has a choice to tap into the Holy Spirit's power to resist the urge to give in to temptation. "No temptation has seized you except what is common to man. And God is faithful; He will not let you be tempted beyond what you can bear. But when you are tempted, He will also provide an escape, so that you can stand up under it" (1 Corinthians 10:13).

❖ Lord, thank You that nothing can separate us from Your love! "For I am convinced that neither death nor life, neither angels nor principalities, neither the present nor the future, nor any powers, neither height nor depth, nor anything else in all creation, will be able to separate us from the love of God that is in Christ Jesus our Lord" (Romans 8:38-39).

❖ Lord, thank You that our salvation is secure and cannot be lost! John 10:27-29 "My sheep listen to My voice; I know them, and they follow Me. I give them eternal life, and they will never perish. No one can snatch them out of My hand. My Father who has given them to Me is greater than all. No one can snatch them out of My Father's hand."

❖ Lord thank you for empowering us to do whatever You call us to do! Philippians 4:13 (AMP) "I can do all things [which He has called me to do] through Him who strengthens and empowers me [to fulfill His purpose—I am self-sufficient in Christ's sufficiency; I am ready for anything and equal to anything through Him who infuses me with inner strength and confident peace.]

❖ Lord, thank You for giving us brothers and sisters all over the world! "Respect everyone, and love the family of believers." 1 Peter 2:17a (NLT).

DICTIONARY OF "SUSANISMS"

Bed-found – This is preferred over "bed-bound" because Susan is not chained to her bed, but these days it is usually where Susan is found.

CareGIVER – Caregivers take care of people. Caretakers maintain houses, buildings, or cemeteries! Susie is my caregiver, and I am hers!

Familyship – The family of God. We prefer "familyship" over "fellowship" because, obviously, we are not all fellows.

Framily – Friends who have become family because of our mutual love for Jesus, our brothers and sisters in Christ which may include our biological family as well.

Full-weight - Susan is not "dead weight" when we lift her because she is very much alive! We are simply bearing her full weight because she cannot assist us.

Remnants – Susan does not call her shortened legs "stumps," because stumps are something you put in a woodchipper. Her legs are "remnants" because Jesus saves and returns for the remnant.

Tater – This is Susan's nickname or job description for Susie. It is short for facilitator because Susie facilitates many things for her.

Finally, PLEASE do *not* refer to Susan as an invalid. She is not IN-valid. Here is her description of herself:

I AM UNIQUELY FIT FOR HIS SERVICE: A DIVINELY DESIGNED PRESENTATION!

INDEX OF SCRIPTURE REFERENCES

Reference	Page
Genesis 3:14-15	22
Genesis 3:15	24
Genesis 12:3	26
Genesis 17:9-14	95
Genesis 17:15-19	26
Genesis 17:17	27, 30
Genesis 17:19	29
Genesis 21:12	29
Genesis 24:43	47
Genesis 28:14	34
Genesis 38	37
Genesis 40:10	36
Genesis 49:10	36
Exodus 13:15	94
Leviticus 12:1-8	95
Leviticus 12:8	92
Numbers 18:16	92, 94
Numbers 24:17a,19a	34
Joshua 1:9	62
1 Samuel 16:7b	106
2 Samuel 7:8-16	44
2 Samuel 7:12-13	38
Psalm 2:7	43, 44, 59
Psalm 22:6-8	104
Psalm 46:10	32
Psalm 103:19	41
Psalm 127:3	63

Psalm 139:13	65
Isaiah 7:14	46, 47, 73
Isaiah 9:6-7	49, 59, 109
Isaiah 11:1	104
Isaiah 11:1-3	38
Isaiah 49:7; 53:3	104
Isaiah 53:7	84
Isaiah 55:9	21, 45
Isaiah 64:8	50
Jeremiah 1:4–5	65
Jeremiah 23:5a	38
Jeremiah 23:5	59
Jeremiah 23:6b	49
Micah 5:2	51, 53
Matthew 1:1	26
Matthew 1:1-2a	29
Matthew 1:2a	34
Matthew 1:2-3	36
Matthew 1:5-6a	38
Matthew 1:18-23	75
Matthew 1:18, 22-25	46
Matthew 1:21	77
Matthew 1:23	47
Matthew 2:10	101
Matthew 2:23	104
Matthew 3:17	43
Matthew 5:14	35
Matthew 6:33	102
Matthew 20:28	68
Matthew 25:21	59

Luke 1:13-15	56
Luke 1:30-31, 34	46
Luke 1:30-34, 38	58
Luke 1:32	43
Luke 1:35-38	61
Luke 1:38	59
Luke 1:41	68
Luke 1:44	65
Luke 1:41-45	63
Luke 1:46-48	68
Luke 2:4-7	79
Luke 2:8-12	81
Luke 2:10-12	84
Luke 2:15-16	87
Luke 2:15-20	90
Luke 2:21-24	92, 94
Luke 2:28-32	97
Luke 2:36-38	99
John 1:1-2, 14	53
John 1:3-4	20
John 1:4-5	97
John 1:29b	85
John 1:46	104
John 3:30	68
John 6:35a	51
John 6:35-48	54
John 7:41-42	105
John 8:12	35
John 8:12; 9:5	54
John 10:7	54

John 14:9	54
John 10:11	90
John 10:11-14	54
John 10:30	44
John 11:25	54
John 14:6, 9	54
John 15:1-5	54
John 17:22	44
Acts 13:32-33	43
Acts 13:33-34	44
Acts 17:6	69
Romans 1:2-3	38
Romans 5:8b	83
Romans 8:1	66
Romans 8:9-11	44
Romans 8:15	44
Romans 8:37	102
Romans 12:9-21	105
1 Corinthians 1:27	69
1 Corinthians 15:20,23	54
2 Corinthians 4:17	102
Galatians 3:6-8,16	26
Galatians 3:16	27
Galatians 3:29	27
Gal. 4:4-5	22,70,92,96
Galatians 4:5	44
Philippians 2:5-8	19
Philippians 2:9-11	49
Philippians 3:10	89
Philippians 3:20-21	85-86

Philippians 4:6-7	50
Colossians 1:16b	36
Hebrews 1:3-5	43
Hebrews 1:5-6	44
Hebrews 7:14a	36
Hebrews 7:25	107
Hebrews 11:17-19	28, 29
James 2	105
1 Peter 3	105
1 John 1:9	37
1 John 3:8b	22
Revelation 1:5	54
Revelation 5:5	36
Revelation 1:17b-18	53
Revelation 11:15b	39
Revelation 13:8b	20, 95
Revelation 22:5a	35
Revelation 22:16	34

NOTES

1. Baker, Warren and Carpenter, Eugene, eds., The Complete Word Study Dictionary: Old Testament, H7886.

2. MacArthur, John, NKJV MacArthur Study Bible, 2nd Edition, note on Psalm 2:7.

3. Sproul, R. C. ESV Reformation Study Bible, note on Isaiah 7:14.

4. Strong, James, The New Strong's Exhaustive Concordance of the Bible, H1035.

5. Baker, H6005.

6. Strong, G1694.

7. Sproul, note on Luke 2:8-12.

8. MacArthur, note on Matthew 2:23.

BIBLIOGRAPHY

Baker, Warren and Carpenter, Eugene, eds., The Complete Word Study Dictionary: Old Testament, (Chattanooga, TN: AMG Publishers, 2003).

MacArthur, John, NKJV MacArthur Study Bible, 2nd Edition, (Thomas Nelson, 1997, 2006, 2019), as quoted on www.biblegateway.com

Sproul, R. C. ESV Reformation Study Bible, (Reformation Trust Publishing of Ligonier Ministries, 2021).

Strong, James, The New Strong's Exhaustive Concordance of the Bible, (Thomas Nelson, 2009).

ABOUT THE AUTHORS

SUSAN SLADE is an ordained minister (Fellowship of Churches and Christian Ministries, now a part of Kerygma Ventures). She earned a BA in English Bible with minors in Pastoral Counseling and Modern Hebrew and a MA in Biblical Literature from Oral Roberts University in Tulsa, Oklahoma. She is the founder and president of Precious Jewels Ministries, Inc., a 501(c)3. She was a guest of "Life Today" with James Robinson. The Lord enables Susan to overcome Cerebral Palsy to serve Him with joy. She previously wrote a devotional book titled A Life's Symphony of Joy and co-authored a year-long devotional titled Let Him In and two shorter books titled Thirty Days of Thanksgiving Praise, and From Prophecy to Perfection: A Treasury of Christmas Devotions with her partner in ministry Susie Hale.

KAREN SUE HALE (SUSIE) has a BA in Music Education and a M.Ed. with a focus on language arts and serves as Vice President and Secretary of Precious Jewels Ministries. In addition to co-authoring books with Susan, she previously had two articles published in "Purposeful Singleness Monthly" and one published on "Christian Women Today," a webzine. Susie taught eleven years at Glenview Christian School in Ft.

Worth, Texas and served as curriculum coordinator there. Susie is Susan's "facilitator" assisting with daily living and more importantly Bible study, making use of her language arts and computer skills.

ABOUT PRECIOUS JEWELS MINISTRIES

The mission of Precious Jewels Ministries is to inspire, educate, encourage, and console the body of Christ and to present the gospel of grace to a lost and dying world. The goal is to minister to pastors, laymen, and new believers through verse-by-verse Bible studies, articles, devotionals, speaking engagements, intercessory prayer, and scriptural blessings. Check out the resources available, order more books, and read devotionals online at:
https://www.preciousjewelsministries.com

You have a story.
We want to publish it.

Everyone has as a story to tell. It might be about something you know how to do, or what has happened in your life, or it may be a thrilling, or romantic, or intriguing, or heartwarming, or suspenseful story, starring a cast of characters that have been swimming around in your imagination.

And at Wyatt House Publishing, we can get your story onto the pages of a book just like the one you are holding in your hand. With professional interior design and a custom, professionally designed cover built just for you from the start, you can finally see your dream of being an author become reality. Then, you will see your book listed with retailers all over the world as people are able to buy your book from wherever they are and have it delivered to their home or their e-reader.

So what are you waiting for? This is your time.

visit us at

www.wyattpublishing.com

for details on how to get started becoming a published author right away.

www.ingramcontent.com/pod-product-compliance
Lightning Source LLC
Chambersburg PA
CBHW070458090426
42735CB00012B/2610